# CELTIC MAGIC

CELTIC
MAGIC
Spellcrafting with the gods and goddesses of the Celtic tradition
MARIE BRUCE
SIRIUS

For Clan Bruce and The Good King,
Robert the Bruce (1274–1329):
a true guiding light then, now and always.

⌘

*Blood of my blood,*

*Bone of my bone,*

*The strength that carries me through,*

*The light which guides me home.*

This edition published in 2026 by Sirius Publishing, a division of
Arcturus Publishing Limited,
26/27 Bickels Yard, 151–153 Bermondsey Street,
London SE1 3HA



ISBN: 978-1-3988-5811-4
AD012864UK

All images courtesy of Shutterstock.

Printed in China

# Contents

Introduction: Cead Mile Failte! 6

Chapter One: Celtic Culture 10

Chapter Two: Celtic Magic 30

Chapter Three: Celtic Deities 48

Chapter Four: Kings and Queens 72

Chapter Five: Warrior Poets 100

Chapter Six: The Otherworld 124

Chapter Seven: Heraldic Beasts and Celtic Creatures 142

Chapter Eight: Celtic Romance 164

Chapter Nine: By Root and Branch, Leaf and Tree 180

Chapter Ten: Wind and Stone 192

Conclusion: Mar sin leibh an-adrasta! 204

⌘

Further Reading 205

Acknowledgements 206

# Introduction

## Cead Mile Failte!

***One hundred thousand welcomes!***

*Failte* or "welcome" to the mystical realms of Celtic Magic. In this book I will share with you the wisdom of the Celts, drawn from the four corners of Britain and the Celtic regions of Scotland, England, Ireland and Wales. Here you will learn more about the ancestry of the British Isles and the proud and powerful race of people known collectively as the Celts.

The Celts are renowned for being an often romantic and sometimes brutal community. In both history and mythology, they have given us many legendary kings and queens, warriors and heroes. From Robert the Bruce and William Wallace to Mary Queen of Scots and Rob Roy Macgregor, Cuchulain (or Cú Chulainn) and Scáthach (or Sgathach), many of Britain's *warrior poets* hail from the Celtic regions. Indeed, the term *warrior poet* itself comes from Irish and Scottish folklore and refers to a chivalrous soldier who fights with *mind, body and spirit*, documenting his deeds in poetry. This lasting legacy remains evident in the literature of the war poets of the last century.

More than that, the Celts were also master magicians and artisans, leaving their sacred artwork dotted around the landscape for us to enjoy and wonder at. Pictish standing stones carved with

intricate Celtic knot work and imagery, such as the Eagle Stone in Strathpeffer, Scotland, still hum with ancient magic. There is a mystery and a magnetism about these stones, imbued by our forefathers, which we can still feel today.

As a Bruce, I have always been deeply drawn to my Scottish Celtic heritage and I have studied the legends, mythology and magic of Britain's Celtic regions for many years. Much of this book is a result of my time spent in Scotland, where the past is very much present and magic flows through the ancestral landscape. There is a tangible feeling of mysticism when crossing the border into any Celtic region, be it Scotland, Wales or Cornwall, which the intuitive naturally feel. To me, it feels like passing through a portal, into a beautiful and enchanted realm.

I want to share this feeling with you in the pages of this book. For those of you who live in the UK, I want to show you how magical a staycation can be, while for those readers who live in other parts of the world, I want to tempt you to visit our sacred Celtic shores. But even if you can't travel to a Celtic country, you will be able to use the teachings of this book to bring the magic of the Clan lands into your own home, wherever you happen to live.

The Celts have much to offer: from them we can learn how to live like warrior poets in our own lives, how to maintain a calm courage in the heat of battle, and how to remain true to ourselves and steadfast in the face of betrayal and adversity.

In *Celtic Magic*, I will show you how to summon the blessings of the Four Winds; how to work spells with heraldic totems,

the Red Dragon, the Red Lion Rampant and the Unicorn; how to invoke Celtic archetypes like Scáthach, the Cailleach and the Morrigan; how to use the symbolism of the Celtic Cross to come to a decision; how to create a Clootie tree in your garden and much more. In this book I have endeavoured to excavate the strands of history, myth and magic, drawn from the heart of Celtic culture and weave them together into a practical guide to modern spell craft, with an ancient Celtic twist.

I hope that you enjoy this journey into the Clan lands of the Celts.

Blessings be upon you,

**Marie Bruce x**

## Chapter One

# Celtic Culture

In ancient times, before the rise of the Roman Empire, the whole of the British Isles were ruled by a single people, made up of many tribes. These people were the Celts. Their influence stretched beyond Britain, far into Gaul, which is modern-day France, Brittany in particular, parts of the Germanic regions and Spain where the Gaels were the predominant Celtic tribe. Great swathes of Europe were under their dominion, and they were the dominant force prior to the Roman invasions.

Much of what we know about the Celts is based on conjecture, speculation, examination of ancient artefacts and educated guess work. Historians and archaeologists have long been fascinated by the ancient Celts, though there is much debate surrounding the topic, including when they first came to settle in Britain. It is thought to have been around 600 BC, though some claim that it was much earlier.

However, one thing they all seem to agree on is that the Celts have left a rich heritage of history, art, music and language that we can explore to gain an insight into our ancient ancestors. For make no mistake about it, there isn't a corner of Britain that wasn't shaped in some part by the Celts. Their sacred stones stand majestically across the land. Their artistic knot-work, skilfully carved into the rock by master craftsmen long ago, still glistens in the rain and frost. The sound of the pipes, once played in the march against Roman armies, now characterises the march into modern conflict zones, such as Iraq and Afghanistan. Then as now, whether they be Scots, Welsh or Irish instruments, when you hear the skirl of the pipes, you know that the Celts have arrived! But just who are the Celts and what place do they have in modern magic?

## Ancient Mystics

The Celts were a pagan culture and like many other shamanic people, they set great store by ceremony and ritual. They wore animal skins, feathers, claws and bones, not just for practical reasons, but also to connect with wild creatures as totems. Even today, you can see many a Scotsman wearing an eagle claw or hawk feathers on his brooch, to hold a ceremonial tartan in place. Vintage sporrans were often fashioned from the heads of animals such as foxes, badgers or wildcats. Totems were a part of the Celtic culture, invoking the spirit of animals to bring about greater cunning, ferocity or wisdom.

There is evidence to suggest that sacrifice was also an aspect of their culture too, and while the modern mind recoils from such a notion, in ancient times, sacrifice of both animals and humans was quite common, as it was thought to ensure the survival of the tribe by giving a life to the gods. These days, the sacrifice made in Celtic magic is symbolic, so you might give a gift of silver to the river to bring about prosperity, or leave an apple at a standing stone as an offering.

# Ancient Tribes

The Celts were a tribal race, often intermarrying and trading with neighbouring tribes – and warring with them too, until the arrival of the Romans gave them a common enemy to fight. From the Caledonii up in Scotland, to the Brigantes in the north of England, to the Trinovantes and Iceni in East Anglia and the Dumnonii in Cornwall, to name just a few, Celtic tribes once lived throughout Britain. They were not just confined to the regions we think of as being Celtic today i.e. Scotland, Ireland and Wales, although we can see echoes of the tribes in the more recent Clan system of those regions.

The arrival of the Romans threatened and ultimately destroyed this ancient tribal culture, and yet we still remember the names of those royal Celts who stood against the Roman invasion – Caratacus, Cartimandua and most notably, Boudicca or Boadicea. These names echo across our own time, heroic by-words for standing against oppression, no matter what the consequences might be. This legacy is their Celtic battle-rage, forever stamped indelibly into our history like the blue woad tattoos Boudicca herself might have worn.

## Princess Scotia – Mother of Scotland

The Medieval origin story of Scotland tells the tale of Princess Scotia or Scota. While there is no real evidence that Scotia actually lived, mythology suggests that she was an Egyptian princess and the daughter of a Pharaoh, Cingris. She was married to a man named Goídel-Glas or Gaythelos, but unfortunately, they were exiled from Egypt after offending the Pharaoh. Together they travelled to Spain, and from there they moved on to Scotland where they had many children who became known as the Gaels, after their father. The area then became known as Scota's land, or Scotia's land, which eventually evolved to become Scotland. It was said that when Scotia fled Egypt, she took her altar stone with her. This was a slab of sandstone that was subsequently passed down through the Celtic tribes to become known as the Stone of Destiny, on which Scotland's kings and queens would be crowned throughout history, right up to the present day when King Charles III was crowned upon the Coronation Throne which was built to hold the Stone, at Westminster Abbey in 2023.

## Ancestral Voices

Like many shamanic tribes, the Celts believed in the power of their ancestors and in a life after death. Archaeologists have unearthed evidence of death rituals, such as sacred last meals and unusually positioned bodies. Many grave goods have also been found, particularly in bog-body burial sites around the UK, where they are preserved by the bog. These grave goods include jewellery, pottery and weaponry, indicating that the Celts believed their loved ones would have need of these items in the afterlife. It also indicates that they continued to feel a close connection with their loved ones after they died and wanted them to have all the comforts of home in eternity.

This focus on ancestral connections is not unusual in shamanic tribes. It is also prevalent in Native American, Mauri, Eskimo and other indigenous tribes. It is an integral aspect of Celtic culture, in that the *past remains present*. By this I mean that the past is regarded as being a part of our own time and not separate from the present day. It is the warp and the weft of the fabric of life, on which our current day-to-day tapestry is being stitched. We are each of us, a thread in the tapestry of our Clan and in the Celtic story as it continues to unfold. This effectively means that you can never be without Clan, for you will always have your Celtic ancestors watching over you and guiding you on your path. You can strengthen this connection by creating an altar or sacred space dedicated to your ancestors.

## Blood and Bone Altar

Find a quiet space in your home to set up an altar to your ancestors. If you are part of a recognised Clan, lay a piece of Clan tartan over the surface as an altar cloth – so I would use the Bruce tartan. If you are not of a Clan, you can use any kind of altar cloth that pleases you. Black is a good choice because it represents the darkness of death and the unknown aspect of the afterlife. Next, light two white candles and place these towards the back of the altar. Now gather together anything that reminds you of your Celtic ancestors – knot-work jewellery, a piece of antler, a dirk, gifts from deceased loved ones, memorial cards – arrange these around the altar. Then place a photo or picture of your ancestors in the middle, between the two candles. This could be a photo of your grandparents or parents, or it might simply be a figure from Celtic history that you feel a strong connection to such as Boudicca, Robert the Bruce or William Wallace etc. Light a stick of your favourite incense in offering and say:

⌘

*By blood and bone*

*By hearth and home*

*I welcome my ancestors to this hearthstone*

*Love wholehearted*

*Though long departed*

*I welcome you in and call you home.*

You can use this altar for your Celtic magic spells, meditations and also to commune with your ancestors for connection and guidance. Remember that you can never be Clan-less, for your ancestors are always there. You are a valuable thread in their tapestry. How you live your life helps to keep the Clan moving forward, at the same time honouring the past and those Celts who have gone before. Even if you are not from a Celtic family, you can still honour the Celts by focusing on the ancient Celtic tribes that resonate most with you.

## Modern Global Celts

Historical events of the 18th and 19th centuries such as the Highland Clearances, the Irish Potato Famine and the Transportations, meant that the more recent Celts travelled far and wide, settling in America, Canada, Australia, New Zealand and so on. This effectively means that there are people all over the globe who can claim a Celtic heritage and so the magic and mysticism of the Celts is an international culture, with many countries, far beyond Scotland, even hosting their own Highland Games each year. So regardless of where in the world you live, you can tap into the ancient magic of the Celts and claim a degree of kinship with them.

## Bagpipes – Weapons of War

It is impossible to think of the Celts without also thinking of the pipes, which are an important aspect of Celtic culture. From the fearsome Carnyx used by the ancient Celtic tribes of pre-history, to the bagpipes that we most commonly associate with today's modern Celtic culture, the pipes have been used for centuries as a musical battle cry and a call to arms.

The piper holds a special place in Clan history. Pipers have always been simultaneously both highly respected by their own people, and greatly feared by their enemies, making them a prime target on the battlefield. If an enemy could take out the piper, they would remove the beating heart of the opposition and morale would plummet. This is due to the fact that the pipes are far more than a musical instrument – they are a tool of power and propaganda. The head of a carnyx looming out of the mists must have been a fearsome sight indeed, enough to make even the boldest of enemies think twice before engaging in battle!

Bagpipes have long been used as a communication device. They were the mobile phones of their time, with merry tunes and funeral dirges being played to relay good and bad news to neighbouring Clans across the glens. As an instrument, they are used to celebrate births, marriages and special events, to make a ceilidh go with a swing and to honour and commune with the Celtic landscape. Witnessing a lone piper *playing to the glen* is a sight and sound to behold, fit to melt even the hardest of hearts.

Moreover, the pipes were also used on the battlefield to instruct the soldiers, giving musical orders to denote when to push forward or fall back, what formations to take and so on. Keeping up the morale of the army was the vital role of the piper – he was the heart of the operation, just as important as the flag under which he played.

This tactical use of the pipes in warfare is the reason they were outlawed after the battle of Culloden in 1745. From then on bagpipes were known as a weapon of war. They are still in use today by the British military, with Pipes and Drums bands playing at regimental events and military tattoos. What is more, they are still used as a battle cry and a warning, with various Scots regiments in recent years, hoisting up their flag and playing the bagpipes as soon as they arrived at Camp Bastion in the combat zone of Afghanistan. A weapon of war indeed.

## Notable Warrior Pipers

- ⌘ **John Macgregor**, known as the Piper of the Alamo, was a Scotsman in America who played to boost morale during a 13-day siege in the Texas War of Independence. Such was his effect on the troops that the general of the opposition sent a message, asking him to stop playing. Of course, Macgregor refused and played on.
- ⌘ **Daniel Laidlaw** was a piper from the First World War. His company was ordered to go Over The Top (OTT) of the trenches, but morale was low due to gas attacks being prevalent and the men were understandably reluctant. Piper Laidlaw went OTT alone and promptly marched up and down the trenches, playing his bagpipes, stirring up the hearts of the men, until they too went OTT and engaged with the enemy forces. For his bravery he was awarded the Victoria Cross.

⌘ **William Millin**, known simply as Piper Bill, was the piper who famously played to keep spirits up during the D-Day landings in the Second World War. He was immortalised with a statue in his honour at Sword in France, to commemorate his courage and contribution to the war.

## HOW TO USE THE PIPES IN RITUAL

While it takes years of study, practice and dedication to learn to play the bagpipes, you can still use them as a tool of power in your own life. Simply download a selection of bagpipe music, or buy a regimental CD, and play it whenever you feel you need a morale boost to raise your spirits. Play the pipes whenever you have a personal battle to fight, be that a health scare, a messy break-up, a toxic work environment etc. Play the weapons of war and allow them to stir up your Celtic courage.

# Phantasms and Psychopomps

The Celts were a very superstitious and otherworldly community of people. They believed in the deep magic of land spirits, ghosts and fantastical creatures. Their world view, mythology and storytelling was populated with phantasms, elementals and spirit animals who could either be helpful, mischievous or malevolent. They would try to communicate with these ethereal beings in rituals, visions or through the medium of a Druid priest or wise woman, asking for guidance, victory in battle and small favours. Some clans had their own *psychopomp* – that is, a spirit animal or totem that was thought to be a guardian of the Clan, or an elemental whose appearance was a warning of danger and doom, such as the Ban Sidhe or banshee. In some cases, the psychopomp was meant to guide a soul safely into the afterlife, or to ward people away from a particular place. For instance, in the Highlands of Scotland there are lots of myths that feature an otherworldly being that makes people feel uneasy when out on the mountains and these spectres could be viewed as psychopomps, warning people of the dangers of venturing too far up the mountain.

## Celtic Meditations and Pathworkings

We will be exploring various phantasms and otherworldly creatures throughout the course of this book using the tool of guided meditation. As the name suggests, a guided meditation takes you on a mental journey, guiding you through an imaginary realm before bringing you back to the current moment in time. This practice is also known as pathworking and it is a bit like daydreaming but with storytelling attached! When using any guided meditation, it is useful to have someone read it out loud to you, or alternatively, you can record it in advance so that you can play it back whenever you want to. Lay down in a comfortable position and close your eyes. Breathe deeply for a while, until you start to feel nicely relaxed, then proceed to visualise as directed.

Each meditation is a chance for you to enhance your psychic abilities and connect with astral beings and ethereal creatures, all with a Celtic theme. In these meditative exercises you can connect with the heroes and heroines of Celtic history and spend time with mythical creatures in your visions to gain insight and guidance for your daily life. These phantasmagorical meditations are designed to take you out of the everyday world and into an ethereal Celtic realm of magic and wonder. You can read them as a relaxation exercise before bed or record them and use them as visualisation tools. Alternatively, you could work with a like-minded friend and read them out to one another.

# Celtic Meditation:
# Chariots of Ire

*You find yourself standing in a valley as dawn begins to break. The air is damp with mist and a chill breeze shivers through you. The atmosphere feels charged and it makes you feel uncomfortable. It reminds you of a situation in your current life where you feel unwelcome and uncomfortable in the presence of someone or something you know. Your anger at the situation is bubbling away inside you. You set off walking through the mist, wrapping your arms around you for warmth.*

*The grass is damp with dew, and you suddenly notice a movement out of the corner of your eye. Turning to look you see that a hare is venturing out into the valley from the cover of the hedgerow. He moves cautiously out into the open, then sits up on his hind legs and scents the air, his nose twitching furiously. His ears stand tall and wide as he surveys the land around him. You stand still, not wanting to startle him. The early morning sun shines on his back, making his grey fur shine like silver in the light. Satisfied that all is well, he drops to all fours and begins to nibble at the grass. Slowly you make your way towards him.*

*"Merry meet, wise one, will you not come closer so that we may be introduced?" you say. The hare looks up at you as if considering your request, then he begins to lollop your way. He sniffs at your feet and rubs his head against your ankles. You suddenly hear a sound away in the distance and all at once the hare streaks off at lightning speed. He senses danger!*

*He runs off, then comes back and circles your feet, agile and swift, before running off again. He is telling you to follow him and so you do. You set off running across the valley back the way you came, unsure of what the danger is but knowing instinctively that it is coming your way. You need to put safe distance between you and the danger that approaches. You run as fast as you can. Glancing over your shoulder you gape at what you see.*

*Coming out of the mist at the far end of the valley are legions of Roman soldiers! The soldiers are marching after you, swords ready to strike you down. You push your legs to move faster as you follow the hare, heading toward the opposite end of the valley. You blink the mist from your eyes and notice a shadowy shape on the horizon. Your ears pick up the sound of wheels and high-pitched squeals. The hare runs ahead of you, guiding you forward. He is heading straight as an arrow, towards the shape in the mist. As you run after him you begin to see that the shadow is none other than a second band of warriors, though these are not Roman. They are dressed in furs and leather armour, their faces painted bright blue. They are Celts!*

*You look around you for somewhere to hide, afraid that you are about to get caught in the crossfire of a great battle. The rumble of wheels comes closer and in a blind panic you turn to run in the opposite direction, back towards the Romans. You don't know where safety is, you only know to run. Somewhere behind you a horse whinnies and the thunder of hooves and wheels rings in your ears. A second later you are swept completely off your feet and thrown down onto a hard wooden surface that rumbles beneath you.*

*"Well met, Seeker!" A woman shouts down to you over the noise. Her red hair is braided tightly away from her face, which is streaked with bright blue woad. In one hand she holds the reins of the horses that pull her chariot and in the other she grasps a long spear. "Are you ready for a war?!"*

*"What?! No! I was just out for a walk; I'm not a part of any war!"*

*"Sometimes Seeker, the war comes to us whether we are ready for it or not. When that happens, we must do battle.* ***You*** *must do battle."*

*"But, why? Who are you?!"*

*"Don't you know me, Seeker? My hare led you straight to me. See how he sits quietly at my feet. He isn't afraid. He has been to war with me many times before and he tells me that we will win this battle."*

*"You're Boadicea?" you say.*

*"Boudicca," she corrects, "Queen of the Iceni. And now you must join in battle and face your enemies."*

*"But I don't have any enemies."*

*"Don't you? Then why do you feel so oppressed, so opposed, so restricted and supressed? Why do you struggle to be heard, Seeker, if there are none who stand against you, none who would benefit from your silence?"*

*You think about this for a moment as Boudicca expertly guides the chariot across the valley, gradually closing the ground between her and the Romans. There are certainly things in your life that have made you feel defeated before – people, organisations and systems in place that seem to be intent on keeping you small and fearful, silent and supressed. Are these the enemies that Boudicca is referring to?*

*"Okay, so there may be a few skirmishes in my life right now, but that's not the same as a war," you admit, reluctantly. After all, no one likes to think that they have enemies, do they?*

*"When you turn a blind eye to the skirmishes, Seeker, you lose the war you didn't even know you were fighting. Here, take the reins!" Boudicca thrusts the reins into your hands, and you feel*

*the sudden tug of the two powerful horses that pull the chariot, suddenly veering off to one side. "Straight!" Boudicca screams. "Keep going straight forwards, Seeker, always forwards. Don't stop or deviate for anyone!" You take a firmer grip on the reins and gently guide the horses back into line, galloping towards the Romans who march ever onwards towards you. "I see the enemy!" she cries. "Battle is joined!"*

*In a flash of chaos, you find yourself driving the carriage straight into the Romans, as Boudicca sweeps her sword from its scabbard and fights with spear in one hand and sword in the other. You marvel at her courage and skill on the battlefield. How you wish you could be more like her! So fearless, so brave and dauntless in the face of war. She swings her spear around you, knocking a Roman from the chariot just before he could strike you with his sword. As you urge the horses on, you begin to feel a sense of exhilaration and excitement. This is what it means to do battle, to stand up to your enemies and face them down, fearlessly.*

*"And now Seeker, it is time. Earn your stripes!" Boudicca thrusts the sword at you, as she takes back the reins and suddenly you understand. You are here to face your enemies, to join them in battle and defeat them in your mind, once and for all. As you grip the sword in your hand you look around at the Romans that surround you. You notice a recognisable face here, an insignia there and you know that these soldiers represent injustice and those who stand against you in your daily life, those who would bully you and show prejudice against you. With a renewed sense of indignation and ire, you fight down your enemies as Boudicca shouts encouragement.*

*"Well done! You missed one. Over here, that's it! Knock them down, Seeker, defeat them in your mind and you will win the war they plot against you! Keep going. Don't give up until victory is yours." Boudicca drives the chariot towards your enemies, as you cut them down one by one – the bully, the system, the injustice, the discrimination, the betrayer – all fall beneath your sword so that they can do you no more harm. It is exhilarating! You feel powerful and victorious. You know that from now on, none shall stand in your way. You will fight your way through every battle life presents to you, with Boudicca's help.*

*At last, there is the sound of a battle horn being blown in the distance. The Romans, those who represent your enemies, are being called to retreat. You have defeated them! Your sword arm is aching as Boudicca pulls the chariot to a halt and smiles at you. "And that, Seeker, is how you win a war! There's fun to be had in battle, is there not?"*

*You smile at her, panting with the effort of the fight. Then Boudicca takes a small pot from her pocket, dips her fingers into the blue woad and paints a Celtic triskele onto your face. "Remember that you are a warrior, Seeker. In life, in peace, in battle and in victory, you are one of* ***my*** *warriors now and I will always be guiding you. I am here whenever you have need of me. I will let my hare show you the way home but know that my sword and my chariot are forever at your service. May your gods go with you." You thank Boudicca for her help and follow the hare down from the chariot, down through the valley and down, down, down, back into your waking life.*

# Chapter Two
# Celtic Magic

Celtic magic is generally regarded as a type of traditional folk magic. It doesn't have the same high ceremonial aspect as Wicca, but it is very effective just the same. While you can cast a circle and call the quarters if you wish, as any Wiccan would do before performing spells and rituals, in Celtic magic this isn't considered necessary as the ancestors are deemed to protect us, rather than the circle. Celtic magic does have some similarities with Wicca and modern paganism, most notably the festival sabbats and you can certainly incorporate some Celtic magic into your Wiccan practice if you want to. There is naturally some overlap, because modern Wicca has its foundation in old traditional folk magic, which the Celts would have been very familiar with.

## Celtic Druids

It is impossible to separate the Celts and Druids, for they were all a part of the same ancient culture. The Druids played a key role in Celtic tribes. They were the recognised religious leaders and spiritual teachers. They were healers, using herbal remedies to tend to the sick and the dying. They were the law enforcers, managing disputes within and between the tribes and ensuring justice was served upon wrong-doers. The Druids were also warriors in their own right, frequently going into battle with their tribe. They were often regarded as Seers or Oracles, using divination to foretell the future of the tribe or warn of ill omens. They were well-known for using a type of divination called augury, which is the art of studying the behaviour and patterns of birds to foresee future events. Other animals could also be used in a similar way. Boudicca, for example, preferred to use the movements of hares and rabbits to foretell if she would win or lose a battle.

The Druids were held in high esteem and were second only to tribal royalty and chiefs. They ensured that the gods were honoured, the festivals observed and the history of the Celts was passed on to future generations. Unlike the Romans however, they were not scribes, and while the Romans documented everything, leaving a written legacy of their time, the Druids and Celts preserved their history through word of mouth, giving rise to one of their most iconic figures, the Bard.

## Bards, Seanachies and Storytellers

The Celtic Bard is a rather romantic figure. We picture him waxing lyrical, holding his audience enthralled as they sit around a huge bonfire in the middle of a misty glen. This image might not be too far from the truth. The fact that this type of activity continued well into the Middle Ages and medieval period, giving rise to the travelling minstrels and troubadours who came after him, would indicate that the Bard was wielding a powerful tool of propaganda and entertainment. It was the Bard's responsibility to ensure that the history of the Clan was preserved in storytelling. He would weave together tales of victory in battle, interventions and signs from the gods, epic romance, encounters with the fey, enchanted weaponry and feats of magic.

Bards were also free to travel, to take the tales of their Clan further afield, to neighbouring Clans. In this way they could act as emissaries and mediators. They would gather news as they went, taking back vital intelligence to their chief, thus playing a key role in the politics, marriages and battle plans of that time. Bards were warmly welcomed and enjoyed a certain amount of protection and privilege, much like the ambassadors of today. They had diplomatic immunity, meaning that they could not be harmed while in the territory of a rival Clan. All this political intrigue was carefully and diplomatically wrapped up in convivial entertainment. Each Clan or tribe would have their own Bard, and these men would have visited rival Clans, which must have made a pleasant change for the audience with an opportunity to hear fresh tales from a new voice, making the deep, dark cold of winter much more bearable.

This Bardic skill has never really disappeared and modern Celts are still renowned for their ability to weave a good yarn. Think of Billy Connolly telling his tall tales on stage to make people laugh, or novelists such as Ian Rankin holding audiences enthralled with his words. The storyteller still plays a significant role in our society, from TV and radio script writers, to authors, poets, musicians and so on. The power of the Bard is still prevalent in modern Celtic society too. Ask any Scotsman for directions and he will give you the history of every landmark you are likely to pass on the way to your destination! The Celts rarely get straight to the point, because they will always have a long tale to tell. That is part of their charm.

# The Mabinogion

It is highly likely that some of the tales told by the ancient Druid seanachie and bards would have come from the Mabinogion, which is a collection of Welsh folklore and mythology. There are four main branches, or sagas of the Mabinogion, and the collection comprises eleven tales in all. These include the stories of Pwyll, the Prince of Dyved, Bran and Branwen, Geraint and Enid, the Lady of the Fountain, Taliesin, the Dream of Mascen Wledig, Culhwch and Olwen, among others.

The myths of the Mabinogion, which loosely translates to *tale* in English, were first collected and written down during the medieval period, when they appeared in two books, *The White Book of Rhydderch* and *The Red Book of Hergest*. Prior to that they would have been passed down via word of mouth, by the storytellers and bards of the time. It is thought that the tales

originated over a period of time and were written by different creators, rather than a single author. In this sense the Mabinogion is akin to the Norse Sagas. It is likely that each author was inspired by and built upon the work of their predecessors, and so the tales grew into the collection we know today.

In the 19th century, the linguistic scholar Lady Charlotte Guest brought all the tales together and published them in a single anthology, under the title of *The Mabinogion*, but the stories themselves are much older, with some of the earliest tales dating from the 1100s. In reading the tales it is clear to see how they became embedded into British storytelling culture, as they feature the famous Red Dragon of the Welsh flag and an early appearance by King Arthur and some of his most famous knights, Geraint and Gawain. It could even be argued that the Mabinogion is the originator of what later became known as the Arthurian Legends, with the Lady of the Fountain being a precursor to Avalon's Lady of the Lake, and that without these classic medieval Welsh tales, legends of King Arthur and his Knights of the Round Table simply wouldn't exist.

While some of the later aspects of the Mabinogion are of a more traditional romantic tone of register, other tales touch on themes of political rivalry, the threat of invasion and colonisation by the English or the Irish, family feuds, tales of revenge and punishment, all embellished with fantastical events, magical interventions and otherworldly creatures.

## The Tale of Geraint and Enid

*Geraint was a knight and he married the daughter of a noble earl. Her name was Enid and she was devoted to her handsome husband. The couple spent so much time together, enamoured by one another's presence, that rumours began to circulate that Geraint had lost his edge, and that his fighting spirit had been dampened by his wife. Obviously, no man wants to be thought of as being under his wife's thumb, and Geraint was no different. He loved his wife, but he also wanted to be a great knight.*

*He feared that his wife had heard the rumours and perhaps believed that he wasn't the fine knight she had envisioned when she first married him. Determined to prove himself to both his wife and his peers, Geraint decided that he and Enid should leave court for a time and travel back to their own castle. He saddled the horses and made ready for the journey, instructing Enid not to speak to him as they made their way back home.*

*Enid was saddened by this, especially as her husband forced her to ride ahead of him. Geraint was so lost in his thoughts that Enid was sure he hadn't seen the fallen tree that lay across the road up ahead. She turned in the saddle and called out to him, disobeying her husband and alerting him to the obstacle. With a curt nod, Geraint dismounted and hauled the log out of the way, once again instructing his wife not to talk to him as they rode on. However, a little later, Enid noticed that there was a beggar crouched in the hedgerow. Convinced that Geraint hadn't seen the beggar, she called out to her husband that perhaps he needed their help. Again, with a curt nod Geraint dismounted and approached the beggar, giving him food, a flask of wine and a few coins. Enid smiled on her husband in satisfaction. He really was such a good, kind man! She could not have done better. He grunted ill-temperedly in reply to her beaming smile.*

*Geraint mounted his horse and instructed his wife not to talk to him for the third time. He could see by now that the rumours were true – she just didn't trust him to take good care of her, or to do the knightly thing without prompting. She too thought that he had lost his edge. They rode on in silence, until once again Enid turned and called out that there was a gang of ruffians lying in wait in the trees and hadn't they better find another way?*

*But Geraint would not be diverted. Instead, he spurred his horse on, galloping ahead of Enid and did battle with the ruffians, defeating them easily. Then he turned angrily on his wife, "Why did you disobey me, wife? Three times, I* ***told*** *you not to talk to me. Did you think I could not see the log, or the beggar? Did you think that I could not detect danger without you pointing it out to me? Why did you not simply* ***trust*** *me?"*

*Somewhat perplexed Enid replied, "But I* ***do*** *trust you! You are the finest knight I know. I only wanted to help you, to support you in your work – that's all. Why do you berate me for being a good wife to you?"*

*Then Geraint threw back his head and laughed at his own folly and pride. He had found a wife who would ride into battle with him if he let her! That was a prize worth holding onto. And so ends this tale of the Mabinogion.*

What is interesting about this story is that it highlights the differences in how men and women might view the same situation. Although there are several versions of the tale, the main theme always remains the same. Geraint, tired of being teased by his peers about his new matrimonial state, feels that he has to prove himself. He wants to test Enid to see how much she trusts him and his knightly prowess. When she keeps alerting him to danger and obstacles, he feels belittled and emasculated. However, in Enid's mind, she is simply offering her support to her husband who has a very difficult job. She feels that she is being a good wife when she alerts him to danger, proving that she is on his side. In the end, they come to an understanding and begin to work as a team. It is a useful moral tale in how to try and see someone else's perspective before jumping to conclusions! There is a wonderful painting of this myth from 1907, entitled *Geraint and Enid* by Rowland Wheelwright, which perfectly depicts Enid's good intentions and Geraint's annoyance!

## Celtic Sabbats

The Celts observed the wheel of the year, honouring the turning of the seasons with a series of eight festivals, which are as follows.

**CALEN GAEAF** *(31 October)* – this is the Celtic new year and the sabbat where we reflect on all that the past twelve months has brought. Ghost stories are a traditional part of this sabbat, as is carving out a turnip. In Cornwall it is also known as *Allantide*, a feast which honours the apple harvest and the cider that comes from it.

**ALBAN ARTHAN** *(21 December, midwinter solstice)* – traditionally this was the sabbat when the Druids would cut down mistletoe and bless it. We still honour this tradition today by hanging mistletoe in the home in December.

**GWYL FORWYN** *(2 February)* – this is the feast of the maiden, usually represented in Celtic culture by the goddess Bride or Bridget. It is a time to welcome back the strengthening light.

**ALBAN EILIR** *(21 March, spring equinox)* – this is the time of the quickening, when the earth begins to show the first signs of spring. At this time, it was traditional to bless the seeds that were to be planted, be this a garden, a crop or a new goal or ambition. Bless the seeds for growth.

**CALEN MAI** *(30 April)* – this sabbat is the feast of the May blessing, a time of union, fertility and coming together to enjoy the warmth and the greening of the earth.

**ALBAN HEFIN** *(21 June, summer solstice)* – at this festival the mead and the whisky would have been blessed as part of a great summer celebration.

**GWYL AWST** *(1 August)* – a feast of harvest and thanks, blessing the bannock/bread that would feed the Celts through the winter months.

**ALBAN ELFED** *(21 September, autumnal equinox)* – this is the time of strengthening darkness and the feast of the Cailleach, who is welcomed rather than feared. She brings the cold depths of winter and feasting in her honour was thought to ensure the survival of the Clan through the winter months.

## PectiWita – The Magic of the Painted People

In the Highlands of Scotland there is a branch of paganism that has been practiced for hundreds of years by the Highlanders. It is known as PectiWita, or Wita. The term originates from the Picts or Picti, meaning painted, which refers to the fact that these people would paint themselves with blue dye from a woad plant. This was illustrated in the classic film *Braveheart*, although William Wallace actually lived much later than the Picts and it is unlikely that he painted his face blue to meet King Edward on the battlefield!

The Picts were a Celtic tribal people from the late Iron Age, who believed in being true to themselves, defending their territory valiantly and upholding a sense of freedom. This sense of freedom still resonates throughout Scotland today and the Scots have a very tolerant 'live and let live' attitude to others. PectiWita utilises aspects of traditional Highland dress, such as swords, sporrans, dirks and targes, as magical tools. I use a dirk as a substitute for the traditional witch's athame and I find that it works just as well, lending a touch of PectiWita to my rituals and connecting me to my Bruce ancestors.

## Practising Celtic Magic

As you can see from this chapter, Celtic magic is very similar to modern Wicca and there might be much that already seems familiar to you or that resonates with you. The main tools used are a dirk, or some kind of blade, and a cauldron for holding fire spells, water etc. As a form of folk magic however, Celtic

magic relies mostly upon the inner power of the soul, of courage, forbearance and connection with nature. Throughout the rest of this book there will be spells, rituals, meditations, invocations and divinations for you to try so that you can connect with the magic of the Celts whenever you choose.

# Celtic Meditation: **Monk's Crossing**

*You find yourself standing on a country lane as dusk begins to fall on a hot day towards the end of summer. You can smell the pollen in the air, warm with a golden haze. It smells like heather and harebells. A full moon has risen before the sun has even fully set, the two heavenly orbs creating an eerie glow across the landscape. On one side of the lane is a copse of trees, while on the other is a deep glen. You set off walking along the lane, enjoying the deepening dusk and the silver moonlight. There is a slight mist hanging in the air, and from the trees an owl calls out for its mate.*

*As you walk, you ponder on a question that has been bothering you for some time. You know that eventually you will come up with an answer, but for now you simply hold the question in your mind. An unearthly shriek behind you makes you jump and turn. You see the owl making its silent flight across the lane and over the glen. "It's just an owl," you say, "Nothing to fear." You continue walking, but all at once you begin to feel a little uneasy. In the distance you can hear some kind of singing. No, not singing, chanting. It's coming from the woods. You stand still for a moment, trying to make out the muffled voices. It's definitely coming closer, the deep rumbling of many voices all chanting together in perfect harmony. You look around to find the source, but there doesn't seem to be anyone around.*

*Then you see it. Just up ahead, at the side of the treeline the mist thickens and swirls, like a curtain. You watch in fascination as the mist seems to dance in the air, the moonlight illuminating it. Then you begin to discern shapes moving in the mist and eventually stepping out of it, dark grey shapes of cowled figures, like monks. No, not just monks, but druid monks!*

*They walk in twos, their grey-white robes glowing in the moonlight. Some walk with their arms tucked into their sleeves and across their bodies, while others swing censers of incense as they go, cleansing the path before them. Two by two, they walk across the lane in front of you and head down into the glen, chanting sonorously as they go. As you gaze at them, you see that they are not fully there, their shapes flitting in and out of the mist, one moment almost solid, the next vaporous and indistinct. Their chanting is otherworldly and that is when you realise that these are no ordinary monks – they are ghosts!*

*Suddenly there are dozens of ghostly druids crossing the road in front of you, chanting as they go. They do not seem to have noticed you at all, with their cowls pulled up over their heads, but you feel that you must speak to them, to let them know that you see them, that you are in awe of the moment that is unfolding before you. You do not feel afraid, for you sense no malice in these druid monks, only a deep benevolence and spiritual calm.*

*Before you can change your mind, you step forward towards them. One of the druids glances your way, then steps out of the formation, allowing his brethren to go on without him. "Merry meet, Brother, it's a fine evening for a stroll," you say.*

*The druid draws back his cowl and smiles at you. "Good evening," he says, "Yes, it is a fine evening indeed. What brings you here, child?"*

*"I am pondering on a question I have wrestled with, and I hoped that a meditative walk would give me some clarity."*

*"Ah, yes, a meditative walk is infinitely good for the soul. My brothers and I often walk this way, yet most choose not to see us, or they see us, and they are afraid. Are you not afraid?"*

*"No. I don't feel any malice in you at all, quite the opposite in fact. What should I call you?"*

*"Call me Brother Fion. I and my brethren are going to a gathering of the Order, to celebrate the full moon. Perhaps you would like to walk with us for a time?"*

*"I would, thank you." You follow Brother Fion as he falls in line at the back of the column of druid monks, the two of you walking side by side and bringing up the rear. After a time, Brother Fion speaks. "Perhaps if you were to tell me your question, I may be able to help you decipher a solution." You confide in the druid and listen to his wisdom as you walk. He helps you to see the situation in a new light, offering insights that you hadn't considered before. You find his company calming and reassuring. He speaks with authority and wisdom, and you are open to listening to his good counsel.*

*"The important thing, child, is that you are careful who you trust. People will always reveal their true nature if you allow them to. Only give them enough time and space and they will show you who they really are, and when they do, believe your own eyes and what you see, not the false promises of those who speak with a silver tongue."*

*"Thank you, I will bear that in mind. But tell me Brother Fion, why do you and your brethren walk this way so often? Why are you not resting in peace?"*

*"We follow the old ways, child, even unto death and beyond. We honour the moon and the seasons, we walk the ley lines and the by ways, keeping the Veil open and guarding the portals. In life we gave ourselves to our faith, and in death we follow the same path."*

*"But are you happy?" you ask, concerned for this kind old spirit.*

*"I am where I am meant to be, whenever I am meant to be there. As are you. We can ask for no greater gift than that. I am content in my calling." The two of you walk on in silence for a time, until the druids come to a Celtic cross set in the path that stretches out across the glen. They form a circle around the cross and the chanting stops. Brother Fion steps in front of you and says "This is as far as you go child. The Gathering is about to begin, and it is not a ritual for the living." He reaches into the sleeve of his robe, takes out a small pouch and hands it to you. "In here you will find the answer to your question. Remember to be careful who you trust and know that I am here, walking the old ways whenever you have need of me." You take the pouch and thank the kindly druid monk, who takes hold of a censer and proceeds to wave it around you. Then in a smog of incense smoke you find yourself drifting down, down, down, back into your waking life.*

## Chapter Three
# Celtic Deities

The Celts believed in a wide range of gods and goddesses. Some of these deities were worshipped in several Celtic regions, for example the Morrigan, who was held in high esteem throughout Scotland, Ireland and Wales. Others were central to a particular region, like Bran the Blessed, one of the Welsh gods of the Mabinogion. Still others were known by different names in different regions but are essentially the same deity. In this chapter we will look at some of the main deities of the Celtic pantheon and how they can be invoked for magical purposes.

## **Cernunnos** – Horned One

Cernunnos is probably the most important Celtic deity there is. A powerful god of forest and animals, he is depicted with antlers growing from his brow. He is seen as the guardian of wildlife and wildwood places. He has been worshipped for thousands of years, his image carved in rock, stone and iron by our primitive ancestors. Perhaps the most famous depiction of Cernunnos is the one on the Gundestrup cauldron, which dates from approximately 150BC – 1BC. This cauldron is a symbol of transformation and regeneration, representing the life cycle of birth, death and rebirth. In terms of magic, Cernunnos is a great all-rounder, and he can be invoked for strength, courage, resilience, fertility, passion and protection. In England he was later known as Herne the Hunter. You can connect with him by spending time with deer, observing them in the Highlands or a deer park. Antlers are naturally shed each year, so adding one to your altar would honour this god. Invoke him with this traditional chant:

⌘

*Hoof and horn, hoof and horn*

*All that dies shall be reborn*

*Cernunnos, Horned One*

*Guide my steps 'till day is done.*

## Arawn – Lord of Annwn

Bearing some resemblance to Cernunnos is Arawn, the Welsh god of Annwn or the Otherworld. He is sometimes depicted with a pair of ram's horns spiralling from his head, rather than antlers and occasionally, with a skull's face to denote his role as Lord of Death. However, this shouldn't make him a fearsome god, for Arawn promises the blessing of an afterlife in Annwn, a land of abundant feasts and eternal happiness. Like Herne, Arawn is a Hunter god, often shown on horseback with a pack of hounds beside him. He is also known as Gwyn ap Nudd and in this aspect, he is said to preside over the fairy realms and fairy portals. Magically he can help you to attune with Elphame or the fairy realms, come to terms with a loss or bereavement, or prepare for the end of something. He is the strength in the sorrow, the hope of a new start following a loss. He should not be feared, but embraced, as he provides the life lessons that we all must learn. Arawn is associated with the season of autumn, as the natural world begins to die back, so attune with him by wearing autumnal colours, walking in the woods, or by blowing a hunting horn or wind instrument. Invoke him with this chant:

⌘

*Arawn, Arawn of spiralled horn*

*Of portals fair 'tween dark and dawn*

*Guide me through each loss I bear*

*I lean on you, your strength to share.*

## The Morrigan – Battle Goddess

The Morrigan is probably the most well-known of the Celtic goddesses. She was worshipped throughout the British Isles, particularly in Scotland and Ireland. Her Welsh counterpart is called Branwen, sister of Bran the Blessed.

The Morrigan is a powerful Triple Goddess. Also known as The Three in One, she shapeshifts from maiden, to mother, to crone and back again, depending on the circumstances. She is by turns, a seductive woman, a wise crone, a mother figure who is all nurturing and giving. She is always a powerful source of protection. As a battle goddess, the Morrigan decides who lives and dies on the battle field and she is particularly drawn to warriors and the military. All members of the crow family are her sacred birds, so ravens, rooks, crows, magpies etc. are her messengers. Should any of these birds' nest in your garden, it is said to mean that the Morrigan herself is watching over your household. However, it is bad luck to feed her carrion birds and doing so can bring about misfortune. Collecting their naturally shed feathers, however,

is a great way to connect with this goddess. She can help with disputes, unfair treatment, abuse, justice, victory and so on. Bear in mind that she has little time for trouble makers, so if the fault lies with you, the Morrigan will see justice served.

To cast a simple spell for her assistance, hold a black crow's feather in your hand and focus on your intention. So you might ask for the protection of your family or property. Hold the intention clearly in your mind, speak it out loud and invoke the Morrigan's assistance with this invocation, then let the feather fly on the wind:

⌘

*Morrigan I call you, hear my plight*

*By crow's feather taking flight*

*What is yours I return to thee*

*I ask your assistance, so mote it be.*

## Andraste – The Victorious

Andraste, also known as Andarta, is the Celtic goddess of victory and achievement. She is thought to have been a deity of the Iceni tribe, meaning that it is possible that Queen Boudicca would have invoked her aid prior to doing battle with the Romans. This is further supported by the fact that Andraste's sacred animal is the hare, which is an animal associated with Boudicca who used their movements as a fortune telling device. Andraste encourages self-discovery and awareness, leading to victory over your own patterns of self-sabotage and negative habits. If you are your own worst enemy, then Andraste is the goddess to invoke for self-mastery. She also teaches the art of patience. You can win any battle you face – but you might not always win at a time of your own choosing. Sometimes you will need to be patience and allow the opportunity for victory to unfold before you. You can call on Andraste whenever you face a particular challenge, or to help you navigate a difficult relationship. Use the following invocation to request her aid and to experience *victory ever after*!

⌘

***Andraste, Andraste***

***Step forth through time***

***Bring your guiding spear***

***Ensure victory is mine!***

## Cerridwen – Cauldron Keeper

Cerridwen is a crone goddess and was very popular throughout Wales and Ireland. She is the keeper of the cauldron of transformation and it is said that Celtic warriors would be taken into her cauldron in death, to be reborn in the afterlife, or resurrected completely. In modern magic the cauldron is still seen as a tool of transformation, with witches burning written spells in a cauldron to bring about manifestation of the magical goal. Cerridwen is the goddess of inspiration, transformation and transcendence. She encourages growth, expansion, learning, but with the caveat that with growth comes change. For a new phase of life to begin, an old one must end. You must be prepared to make sacrifices to experience transformation. Call on Cerridwen to help you with any period of change, for inspiration, growth, renewal or transformation of your life. Do this by writing your goal on a slip of paper and burning it in a small cauldron as you say:

⌘

*Cerridwen, cauldron keeper*

*Take this desire true*

*Transform it in your cauldron*

*Make all that was renew*

## Cyhiraeth – Bringer of Change

Cerridwen isn't the only goddess of transformation. Cyhiraeth is the goddess associated with change and metamorphosis. She is a symbol of the changing seasons, the ageing process and changes in circumstances. She can't abide a stagnant situation, so if you don't take steps to go with the flow naturally, this is the goddess who will bring about enforced change to shake you out of your rut! Cyhiraeth wants to show you that change is magical and that it usually leads on to something better in the long run. It might not always seem that way, but given time, all changes will eventually lead you to exactly where you are meant to be. Change is a universal tool of ascension. It isn't something to be feared, but should be embraced, because it indicates that you are growing into a new version of yourself. If you struggle with accepting change, or you feel stuck in a rut, call on Cyhiraeth to smooth out the process for you with these words.

⌘

*Cyhiraeth, I accept all things must change*

*So turn and turn about*

*Help me to accept the strange*

*Let blessings flow in and out.*

## Brighid – Light Bearer

Brighid is the Irish goddess of hearth and home. Also known as Bride, Bridget and Brigantia, she is the sacred flame of the hearthside, the heart of family life. As a goddess of spring, she brings the light back after a long winter and the sabbat of Gwyl Forwyn is her sacred festival. Brighid is also a patron of poets, writers, bards and singers. Her energy is light, bright, loving and joyful. Invite her into your home by making a space for her, traditionally called Bride's Bed. Place a small chair, stool or cushion by the hearth – or the warmest spot in the house – and say:

⌘

*Blessed Brighid I welcome you*

*Keep safe this hearth and home*

*Let your sacred fire burn*

*That none shall feel the cold*

*Welcome Bride!*

# Bran and Branwen

Bran, meaning raven, is a sun god in the Celtic pantheon, while his sister Branwen, represented the moon. Both these deities feature strongly in Welsh folklore. When Branwen was mistreated by her husband the king of Ireland, Bran exacted revenge in a great battle. There he rescued his sister, but he was struck with a poisoned dart during the battle. He gave orders that his head was to be removed and buried at the site that is now the Tower of London, where his sacred ravens still reside. Bran is a symbol of wisdom, prophetic dreams and augury, while Branwen represents resilience, forbearance, and courage in adversity. Together they are the epitome of family bonds and support, so invoke their aid with this chant if you need to increase your personal support system:

⌘

*Bran the blessed and Branwen strong*

*Shape and form my family bonds*

*Stick together through thick and thin*

*As a family, we will win.*

## Aenghus – Swan Lord

Aenghus (Angus) is a god of love. In Wales he was known as Mabon, after whom the autumnal sabbat in Wicca is named. His festival is the sabbat of Gwyl Awst in Celtic magic. Aenghus is a gentle god of romance, love, healing and water. He is said to guard the watery portals to the Otherworld and he can transform himself into a swan, in order to move among humans undetected. Like the swan, he is a symbol of pure lasting love and successful partnerships. All water birds are under his protection, but swans and swan feathers are a sign that he is close by, casting his love magic on unsuspecting mortals! To invoke the romantic powers of this god, kiss a swan feather, then keep it close to your heart and say:

⌘

*Swan love, pure love, lasting embrace*

*I dream of the Swan Prince, his strength and his grace*

*Calling sweet Aenghus, god of romance*

*Send me a lover for life's longest dance!*

## Druantia – Druid Queen

As her name suggests, Druantia is a goddess of the Druids and she is sometimes referred to as the Queen of Druids. She is a goddess of the trees, forests and nemeton glades and she is associated with dryads, forest nymphs and other nature spirits of the woods. Some believe that it is this goddess who created the Celtic tree calendar and gifted it to her druid followers, similar to Odin discovering the Nordic runes and sharing them with the Vikings and Norse people. Traditionally she communicates through leaves, so if a leaf blows towards you, it is a sign that Druantia is close by, and she is sending you her blessings. Like Cernunnos she is a guardian of the forest and oversees the growth cycle of the natural world. She is the bringer of peace and serenity you find when you are out in nature and her gift is that of silence, with only the sounds of nature for company. You can invoke her with these words whenever you have need of some quiet time in nature, so make sure that you are outside, preferably near trees, when you use this invocation.

⌘

*Druantia, Queen of the Nemeton Glade*

*Bring me the peace I crave*

*Druantia, lady of leafy shade*

*To chaos I am no longer a slave.*

## Dagda – Staff and Harp Bearer

Dagda was a king of the Irish pantheon of deities that is collectively known as the *Tuatha Dé Dannan*. He was a fearsome warrior who fought with a magical staff, though in some versions the staff is replaced with a mace or a club. Mythology states that the two ends of Dagda's staff could perform different acts of magic, with the rough end ensuring death to Dagda's enemies and his victory in battle, while the smooth end could bring the dead back to life simply by gently touching the body. In this sense Dagda holds similar powers to the Welsh goddess, Cerridwen, and her transformational cauldron. Dagda used his staff to resurrect his own son, Cermait. In some versions of mythology, Dagda is said to be the husband of The Morrigan. Along with his staff, he was also in possession of an enchanted harp that was made from oak and which had two names, *Summer* and *Winter* or *Daur Da Blao* and *Coir Cetharchair*. When Dagda played his harp, he moved the seasons on or brought them back into alignment. He is associated with fertility, abundance, harmony and the power of the seasons. Use the following invocation to call on his assistance:

⌘

***Dagda, father of all seasons***

***Bring me your gifts of plenty***

***Shower me with your abundance***

***Over my wealth, stand sentry.***

## Epona – Horse Goddess

Epona, or Rhiannon as she was known in Wales, is a goddess of horses, fertility, travel and liberty. As you would expect, all equines are sacred to this goddess and the Celts very much depended on their mounts, so it is natural that they should have worshipped a horse goddess. The chalk horses carved into hillsides in England could be a remnant of this kind of worship. Sometimes depicted as a horse, at other times shown as a rider, the goddess Epona was so important in Britain that the Roman's actually adopted

her as one of their own goddesses. In her darker aspect she is the fearsome Nightmare, who forces you to face your fears as you sleep. Sleep is one of her teaching tools and dreams are how this goddess communicates. To attune with her, spend time with horses, go riding, give to an equine charity or help out at a stables. Being around horses can be very therapeutic. They are a symbol of freedom, travel and liberty. To bring the energies of this goddess into your life, find a lucky horseshoe for your altar and chant:

⌘

*Epona, Epona teach me to ride*

*A life of adventure from which I won't hide*

*Obstacles cleared, the past left behind*

*As I go on this journey my fate now to find.*

## Study Celtic Mythology

These are just a few of the Celtic deities. There are many, many more. Studying the mythology of the Celts will introduce you to more gods and goddesses that you might choose to work with. Remember to hold your intention firmly in your head and heart as you request a deity's assistance. You can invoke these gods and goddesses to make your life run more smoothly and to give you a magical edge. Just remember to always be respectful, do your research when working with new deities and find different ways to connect with them that works for you.

# Celtic Meditation: **Hoof and Horn**

*You find yourself standing deep in the Caledonian forest. The Scots Pines tower above you, creating majestic halls of trees and filling the air with their sharp scent. It is midwinter and the snow is falling all around you, settling on the forest paths and making the boughs of the trees hang low, heavy with their burden of snow. You gaze in wonder at the beautiful landscape, which sparkles like diamonds in the glimmers of sunlight that sneak into the forest between the trees. The virgin snow glistens and after a moment or two you feel the childish urge to make your mark on the pristine path before you.*

*You set off walking, your feet sinking into the soft snow flurries, making a satisfying crunching sound as you go. Oh, is there anything better than the first snowfall of winter?! You can't imagine anything better than this right now. The winter forest is bright and gleaming, with the odd cache of red berries hanging from the occasional holly bush. A dainty robin flits from branch to branch, stopping every now and then to fluff up its feathers against the cold, before flying off once more in search of food. The cold air nips at your nose and puts roses in your cheeks, as your breath clouds in the air before you.*

*As you walk on, you take in all the beauty that surrounds you. This is a magical winter forest; you have no doubt about it! It is mesmerising. You can feel the enchantment in the air, and you know that something wonderful is to be found here. You don't know what it is yet, but you trust that all shall be revealed to you when the time is right. You come to a halt at what appears to be a fork in the path. Which way should you go? You're not sure and standing there undecided, you glance around. A rustle in the undergrowth catches your attention and you look over to the side of the snowy path to see what is making the noise. You can't see anything, but the shrubs are moving, and you know that someone is there. "Hello?" you call out into the clear winter air, your voice almost echoing in the cold. The shrub stops moving and you call out again, "Hello? Will you not show yourself to me? I mean you no harm."*

*All remains still and silent for a few moments, then the shrub begins to move again, and a small creature comes out from beneath the undergrowth. It is long and slim, low to the ground as it moves on tiny legs. Its face is pointed, with long silky whiskers and its tail is fluffed up against the cold. Its fur is pure white, and it almost blends right into the snowy landscape, but for the black tip to its tail, by which you recognise it. It is a stoat! A pretty little stoat in its winter white coat.*

*"Merry meet, little one. Are you enjoying the winter weather too?" you ask. The stoat walks over to where you stand and looks up at you, twitching its whiskers. "I was just trying to decide which way to go," you say, "Do you think you could give me a clue?" The stoat gives a nod and turning round, it heads off down the right-hand path, with you following behind. The stoat moves swiftly and gracefully, its tail swishing through the snow as it goes. You keep your eyes fixed firmly on the black tip of its tail, as the white stoat leads you deeper and deeper into the forest. Here the woodland is much thicker, and you have to push branches to one side so that you can get through. You push against bough after bough, each*

*one leaving a deposit of snow on your head and shoulders, until you are soaked through, but finally you find yourself in a small clearing in the woods and what you see before you, takes your breath away and makes you gasp in delight.*

*A bevvy of doe is standing in the clearing, each one munching on some much-needed food: apples, acorns, berries, oats etc. The snow is falling onto their slender backs, turning their tawny brown fur white and frosty. Their ears are set wide apart on their heads, forever twitching, alert to any sign of danger, but they do not seem troubled by your presence. Some stare at you with large, trusting brown eyes and the cheeky flick of a scut-tail. There must be thirty or forty deer here in the clearing and they are beautiful, but it isn't the doe that made you gasp.*

*There in the centre of the grove stands a man. He holds open a sack from which he is throwing food to the doe, but that isn't what made you gasp either. This man is like no other man you have ever seen in your life! He is very tall, bare chested despite the snow, and you can see that he has tattoos of blue woad painted across his chest and arms. His hair is long, mixed with autumn leaves of bronze, copper and gold. It hangs in tawny brown and chestnut waves that fall softly to his shoulders, similar in colouring to the doe that surround him and who clearly adore him. You can see why – for growing from his brow is a magnificent pair of antlers! Not a headdress of any kind, but actual antlers of his own, growing proudly from his head. Furthermore, his legs are not those of a man, but those of a deer, with cloven hooves instead of feet! He is one of them – both a stag and a man combined! He is amazing and you are awestruck by his magnificence, his obvious strength*

*and otherworldly beauty. There is the silvery ringing of magic in your ears each time the stag-man moves.*

*In a flash of white the stoat runs up to the man and leaps around his legs, until the man turns and spots you standing on the edge of the clearing. He grins in welcome and motions you to come closer. "Merry meet, Seeker!" he says, "I see you have met my friend, Skurry. Has he led you a merry dance?" he asks as he leans down to stroke the stoat's back.*

*"He guided me here," you reply, "To you."*

*"And do you know to whom you speak, Seeker? Do you know who I am?"*

*"Yes. You are Cernunnos, of the Old Ones."*

*"I am indeed. Come and meet my ladies. I like to keep my girls happy through the winter, when the snow is deep and the nights are cold, I offer them all the gifts of my abundance and protection. Here, you feed them and get to know them better." Cernunnos hands you the sack of food and you busy yourself throwing carrots and apples to the doe. As they come to trust you, you are able to pet them and enjoy their company.*

*"Lovely creatures, doe," says Cernunnos. "Timid mind you, but once they trust you, they will adore you for life. You just need to take your time with them and get to know them gently. You can't rush a doe – try it, and she'll give you a good kick!" Cernunnos's bellowing laugh rings throughout the clearing.*

*"Thanks for the tip. I'll remember that." You empty the last of the food onto the floor and fold the sack neatly, giving it back to Cernunnos. "But where are all the stags?" you ask.*

*"The bachelor herd will be along later. The doe always come in with the first snow. Dainty creatures, they are. The stags are hardier. And what brings you here, Seeker? Troubles that have plagued you? Griefs you need extra strength to bear? Needing protection, maybe? Or something else?"*

*"No, nothing like that," you say, "But my life feels so mundane. I would like to be more open to magic. I want my life to feel like all of this! This place –it's filled with enchantment! I could feel it as soon as I stepped into your forest. I want my own life to feel like this. I want more... I don't know, more enchantment, I suppose."*

*"Enchantment, eh? Always a tricky one is enchantment. Now if you'd asked for fertility, virility, abundance – that's easy. I could offer that to you in a heartbeat. But enchantment – that's a bit more complicated."*

*"Why? What makes it so?"*

*"Well, because much of the enchantment has already been lost in your world, Seeker. You are asking for something that once was there, but now is less so, and you would have me make it more so, yes?"*

*"Yes, please, Cernunnos. I would have you make it more so."*

*"Mmmm." Cernunnos folds his arms and fixes you with his steady, brown-eyed gaze. "Let me ask you this, Seeker. What does*

*enchantment mean to you? How will you know when I have granted your request and made your life more enchanting? What would be different?" You think for a moment and explain to Cernunnos what you mean by enchantment and what magic you would like to see more of in your life. "Those are all very good examples, Seeker, but nothing that I haven't already given you."*

*"What? What do you mean?" you ask.*

*"The enchantment you long for is already there in your heart, Seeker. You are the only one who can transfer it into your life." You ponder on this for a time, and you realise that Cernunnos is right. There is enchantment and magic in your heart, that is why you see it so clearly reflected in the winter forest. You just need to tap into it. You gaze at your snow-laden shoes wondering how you should proceed.*

*Cernunnos shakes his head and sighs, "Look Seeker, I'll make you a deal. I'll give you an extra boost of enchantment, but you must promise me that you will find ways in which to share it with the rest of the world. Bring it out into the open. Offer it to your loved ones and so on. Become the light of enchantment you wish to see in your world. Deal?"*

*You smile in relief. "Deal," you agree and shake hands on it. Then Cernunnos turns around. "Follow me Seeker, I've got something for you over here." He leads you to the foot of a mighty Scots Pine, where you see a large cauldron nestled into the roots. Cernunnos grins at you, "I borrowed this from Cerridwen and she'll have my hide if I don't return it soon. I must have known you were coming, Seeker. Now, see the snow in the cauldron?" You nod. "Take a handful and blow it into the air as you focus on the kind of enchantment you want in your life and which you will share with the world."*

*Crouching down you scoop up a large handful of snow from the cauldron, pause for a moment, then close your eyes and blow it away as you make your heartfelt wish. "Excellent!" says Cernunnos, clapping you on the back. You can see that the snow you just blew away has turned into silver dust, sparkling through the air amid the snowflakes. "There is your enchantment, Seeker, on its way to your life. Now, remember your promise, to share it well."*

*"I will. Thank you, Cernunnos, for your help."*

*"I am always here for you, Seeker. You can find me in my enchanted forest whenever you have need of me. But now it is time for you to go back to your own realm."*

*"How? Will Scurry lead me home?"*

*"No, I know another way." Cernunnos knocks three times on the wood of the Scots Pine tree and a bright light emerges from it as a door opens in the trunk. "Step through the door, Seeker, and it will take you home." You thank Cernunnos once again, then step through the door, into the heart of the tree, where you find yourself sinking down, down, down through the roots and back into your waking life.*

## Chapter Four

# Kings and Queens

**In Britain we have a long history of monarchy. Right from the earliest Celtic queens and the famous battles of Medieval kings, we have a very regal past. Some of these royal figures have become legendary, icons in their own right and people we still admire and talk about centuries later.**

## Two Queens, One Problem

When the Romans invaded Britain, the Celts faced a difficult dilemma: live in peace but under Roman rule, with the possibility of being forced into slavery and made to fight Roman wars. Or fight the Romans to try and maintain control of their own island and their tribal way of life. Two Celtic queens handled this dilemma in very different ways.

Boudicca was queen of the Iceni tribe. After the death of her husband, the Romans, being a patriarchal society, refused to recognise her as queen and came to take over her lands. When Boudicca refused to give up her royal claim and homelands, the Roman's flogged her for disobedience and raped both her daughters, mistakenly believing that this would bring Boudicca to heal. It didn't. It roused her rebel heart and she took revenge on the Roman's by leading an army of Iceni and Trinovante warriors and sacking the city of Camulodunum, which is modern day Colchester. From there she moved on to Londinium (London) where she repeated the victory. Ultimately though, Boudicca was defeated and disappeared from history. Some say that she died of her injuries or illness, while others claim that she took poison so as not to live under Roman rule. Whatever the truth may be, she certainly gave the Romans a sting they didn't forget, and in documenting her name and victories, they left behind her legacy of rebellion, to be poured over by scholars and historians for years to come. Centuries later we still say her name with admiration and Boudicca has become a legendary figure, striding though history, standing against oppression. Today, a statue commemorating her courageous victory stands in London, near Westminster Bridge.

Further north, Cartimandua, queen of the Brigantes, took a very different tactic when it came to the Romans. She became their ally. Cartimandua believed that the best way to ensure the survival of her tribe was to merge it with the new governing force via trade and a common understanding. In this way, she hoped to maintain some control over her lands and her people. The tactic worked for some time and the Brigantes and Romans seemed to co-exist together quite successfully – until Cartimandua divorced her husband, which led to him arranging a rebellion against both Cartimandua *and* the Romans. While the rebellion failed the first time, the second one was more successful and Cartimandua had to be rescued by Roman soldiers. At this point she disappeared from history and no-one knows what happened to her, but her decision to ally with the Romans made the Brigantes one of the wealthiest, most successful tribes in ancient Britain.

Both these queens demonstrate that a sense of freedom was, and still is, incredibly important to the Celts. While Boudicca and Cartimandua had different tactics for dealing with Roman invasion, they both had the same goal, which was to maintain a sense of autonomy and control over their own destiny and that of their people.

## Boudicca Spell to Stand Against Oppression

On the night of the full moon, take a black candle and carve into the wax the nature of the oppression you are facing. This could be racism, bigotry, workplace bullying, sexism, harassment etc. On the other side of the candle carve Boudicca's name. Hold the candle in your hands and picture Boudicca fighting the Romans from her war chariot. Now change the visualisation so that you are standing in the chariot, defeating those who oppress you, with Boudicca by your side. When you can see this image clearly in your mind, light the candle and say the following chant three times, then allow the candle to burn down. Repeat the spell each full moon until the oppression stops and work with the meditation in Chapter One, Chariots of Ire. Wear her hare totem for extra connection.

⌘

*I call on Boudicca, Iceni Queen*

*To strengthen my resolve*

*I am not alone, she fights with me*

*Oppression is now dissolved*

*From her chariot I will fight*

*Her valour helps me shine*

*Those who target me now take flight*

*For victory is mine!*

*So mote it be.*

## Cartimandua Spell for Negotiation

Sometimes you have to ask for what you want. Take a tip from Cartimandua and negotiate your way to a better deal. This spell could be used before a job interview, or a meeting to discuss a promotion or a pay increase. If you are buying a big ticket item, such as a new car, cast this spell to ensure you get a good deal. Take two slips of paper and on each one write the positive outcome you are going to negotiate for, say a pay increase, or better working hours etc. Hold them both to your heart and say:

⌘

*Cartimandua, Brigantes Queen*

*I summon your skills from beyond the Unseen*

*Help me negotiate a better deal*

*Speak with my voice to make my goal real*

*Lend me your wisdom, your ruthless drive*

*To take on the challenge and ensure that I thrive.*

*So mote it be.*

Burn one slip of paper in your cauldron, sending your goal out into the universe and keep the other with you until you have negotiated your new reality. Good luck!

## Scáthach – Warrior Queen

Far to the north, on the Isle of Skye, lived the Celtic queen, Scáthach, pronounced Skaaha. Although a Scots queen of the Highlands, Islands and Caledonii regions, she was strongly allied with the Irish tribes as well. Her fortress of Dun Scaith on Skye was long since built over, and it is now the ruins of Dun Sgathgaich. It was here that both Scots and Irish warriors would be sent for training, because Scáthach was far more than a simple queen – she was a warrior queen who trained the elite soldiers of her time. Young men would have to scale the walls of her fortress to prove that they were worthy of her training.

Scáthach was a battle queen, skilled in all the arts of war, from strategy and negotiation, to physical combat with sword, spear and hand to hand grappling, or what we would now refer to as martial arts. The fact that her name means *Shadowy One* would also indicate that she had skills in infiltration, extraction and assassination. She was not a queen to be messed with!

Scáthach is perhaps most famous for training Cucullainn, also known as the Warrior of Ulster, who eventually became her champion. It is thought that she had a romantic relationship with him too, but he later betrayed her with another woman, for which she banished him from Skye. Still, to this day the island bears his name in the form of the Cullian mountains, so his influence lingers on.

The relationship between Scáthach and Cucullainn is one of the most complex and romantic in Celtic folklore. While the Irish continue to tell stories of their great Ulster hero, in the Scottish Highlands and Islands, it is his tutor, Scáthach who holds all the glory and who is recounted with admiration.

## Scáthach Spell to Get Over a Betrayal

Being betrayed by someone you love and trust is one of the most devastating experiences. It can leave you feeling lost, cut adrift, as if everything you thought you knew is a lie. It robs you of the future you once envisioned. Whether the betrayal comes from a lover, a best friend or a co-worker, betrayal of any kind hits hard and leaves a deep wound. Use this spell invoking Scáthach to help you to move through the pain and into peace of mind. Take a sheet of paper and cut it into a heart shape. On the heart write the nature of the betrayal in red pen. Allow yourself to feel whatever comes up for you as you do this. Take your time with it, holding the heart and absorbing what this betrayal now means for your future. When you feel ready, invoke Scáthach's strength of will, to help banish the traitor from your life and your heart.

⌘

*Scáthach, queen of Skye*

*Betrayed is my heart, blinded my eyes*

*Now I see what once was hidden*

*Through lies and deceit the truth was bidden*

*Give me strength to heal my heart*

*To fight this war as trust departs*

*Banish the traitor, get them gone*

*Free me at last, to start moving on*

*So mote it be.*

Tear the heart to shreds and add the pieces to a fire, for closure.

## Triple Queens Protection Spell

If you ever feel yourself under threat or in an unsafe situation, call on all three ancient queens of the Celts for their protection, by saying the following invocation.

⌘

*Boudicca, Cartimandua, Scáthach, Circle round*

*Guard and protect me from all harm around!*

*Keep me safe wherever I roam*

*Guide my steps, lead me home.*

*So mote it be.*

## Robert the Bruce – King of Scots

Ask anyone in Scotland who *The Good King* is and they'll say Robert the Bruce. Robert I was King of Scots from 1306–1329, but his claim to the crown was not without dispute and his road to the throne was rocky, to say the least!

When King Alexander III died after a fall from his horse in 1286, and his successor the Maid of Norway drowned on her way to claim the throne, the crown of Scotland was up for grabs. Edward I, King of England, quickly claimed overlordship of Scotland. This didn't go down well with the Scots and years of bloody battles followed as the Scots tried to reclaim their country.

Robert the Bruce had a strong claim to the crown, but there was also another claimant – John Comyn, from the powerful Clan Comyn, which held vast swathes of the Highlands. The two men agreed to meet at Greyfriars Kirk in Dunfries, to discuss the best way forward, but an argument ensued and the Bruce killed his rival. From then on it was a race to get crowned and accepted as King of Scots. The Scottish church backed his claim, but Clan Comyn were understandably set against him – inciting a rivalry and blood feud that continues to this day. After many skirmishes, the Bruce eventually won his crown, ultimately sealing his place as king with his great victory at the battle of Bannockburn in 1314.

None of this would have been possible if the Bruce hadn't followed his ambition. He made mistakes along the way and deeply regretted killing Comyn, but his years on the throne led to a more prosperous and independent Scotland, free from English rule. For that he will always be known as *The Good King*.

## Tomb Tabard

During the time that Edward I had set himself up as overlord of Scotland, following the death of Alexander III and the drowning of the Maid of Norway, Edward played a very cunning political game. He proposed that he should oversee the choosing of the next King of Scots, as there was more than one claimant to the throne. That way, he insisted, he could make a fair and unbiased judgment as to who would be the better candidate for the crown. This was meant to keep the peace and prevent all hell from breaking loose as the rival claimants fought it out among themselves!

However, unbeknownst to the Scots, Edward I had set his sights on the throne of Scotland himself. To appease the Scottish people and to further his own ambitions, he proposed that John Balliol, who was related to Clan Comyn by marriage, should be the new King of Scots. Balliol was duly crowned in 1292 and Edward could congratulate himself on now having the powerful Clan Comyn in his debt, having advanced their kinsman to the throne.

Edward's choice was politically strategic because Balliol was known for being a rather weak character. He certainly didn't have what it took to stand up to such a force of nature as Edward I and so he was king in name only. Balliol didn't hold any real power and Edward I ruled Scotland through his chosen puppet king. This didn't go down well with the Scottish nobles, who went behind their king's back and formed a treaty with France, Edward I's sworn enemy. This treaty is now known as the *Auld Alliance*. In reprisal, Edward had Balliol summoned to London, where he was forced to abdicate and imprisoned in the Tower of London, before being exiled from Britain altogether. Edward then invaded Scotland, determined to take the throne by force and the Scottish Wars of Independence began in earnest.

John Balliol became forever known as *Tomb Tabard*, or empty shirt, meaning that he had all the trappings of authority and kingship, but he wasn't fit to rule, being too weak and easily influenced by a stronger power. His role as a puppet king was disastrous for Scotland, giving Edward I the foot in the door he needed, but it did help to clear the path and pave the way to the throne for Robert the Bruce.

## HOW TO RECOGNISE A TOMB TABARD

Society is full of tomb tabards and there are people in all walks of life who cannot accurately, or fairly, wield the power they have been given. In a world where nepotism is rife, it can sometimes seem as if only those who have the right connections can get ahead, while those who are actually the best candidate for the job get left behind. Bear in mind though, that it was only *after* the disastrous leadership of Balliol, that the Bruce's claim was supported and he ultimately led his country to a much better position on the global stage. That said, it can serve you well if you know how to spot false power and how to recognise a tomb tabard when you see one, so here are the clues to watch out for and to help you identify false power.

⌘ **Grandiosity** – they make huge claims about their achievements and experience, with no evidence to support it.

⌘ **Indignation** – they become indignant whenever their authority or ideas and suggestions are questioned.

- ⌘ **Borrowed Plumage** – they take power from others, then present it as their own.
- ⌘ **False Promises** – they will promise you the moon and the sun, but never deliver either!
- ⌘ **Appearance is Everything** – they are more focused on how things look than on actually doing a good job.
- ⌘ **Micromanaging** – they don't let anyone else take charge, even if someone is better qualified or has more experience – *especially* if someone is better qualified or has more experience because they don't want to be shown up! They like to micromanage everyone because that is the best way for them to hide their weak leadership – by dictating to others how things should be done.
- ⌘ **Duplicity** – they are two-faced by nature and you will never get a straight answer from them.
- ⌘ **Sycophantic** – they fawn over those in higher authority, the better to glean favours for themselves, while sneering at those they view as being inferior.
- ⌘ **Absent in Crisis** – when the proverbial hits the fan, they are nowhere to be seen, leaving others to attend to the crisis. Once the situation is back under control, however, they may reappear and take all credit for managing the crisis.

## Marjorie Bruce – Mother of Kings

Although never a queen herself, Marjorie Bruce is extremely important historically and politically. As the eldest daughter of King Robert the Bruce, the princess was of high political value. During the Scottish Wars of Independence, King Robert attempted to send his sisters, wife and daughter to safety, under the watch of his brother, Nigel, but they were soon tracked down by English forces. They sought sanctuary in a small chapel at Tain in Ross-shire, Easter Ross, but they were cruelly betrayed by the Earl of Ross, an ally of Clan Comyn, who handed them straight over to the English soldiers without a pang of remorse.

Marjorie was then separated from her family members, who were all taken and held in different English castles or convents, with Marjorie being held at Watton Abbey in Yorkshire. It is thought that Edward I ordered a special cage to be made for Marjorie as part of her captivity, similar to the one her aunt, Mary, was being held in at Roxburgh Castle, though whether Marjorie was actually confined to the cage within the Abbey or not, we'll probably never know. Her uncle, Sir Nigel Bruce, was named a traitor and suffered a traitor's death, being hung, drawn and quartered at Berwick Castle, as a result of Ross's betrayal. Make no mistake about it, Edward I was sending a clear warning to Robert the Bruce not to oppose him!

Marjorie was held captive in Yorkshire until her father gained victory at Bannockburn, when he demanded his wife, daughter and sisters should be returned to him in exchange for the English lords he had taken prisoner during the battle. She was later married to the Bruce's High Steward and went to live with her new husband at Renfrew. Tragedy struck when Marjorie was thrown from her horse while she was heavily pregnant. The child, named Robert, survived, but Marjorie broke her neck and died as a result of the fall. Her baby was born posthumously by caesarean birth.

However, Marjorie's legacy lived on, and her son became Robert II, King of Scots (1371–1390), being the first of the Stewart line of kings, so named after his father's official role as High Steward in Robert I's court. Marjorie is laid to rest in her tomb at Paisley Abbey, and although she has become little more than a footnote in history, she was in fact the mother of all the Stewart Kings and Queens. As such, there is a memorial cairn built at Knock Hill, Renfrewshire, to mark the spot where poor Marjorie fell from her horse on that fateful and fatal day.

## The Rebel Heart

If there is one thing that the Celts are known for, Robert the Bruce included, it is their rebel hearts! In Celtic culture having a rebel heart is no bad thing. It depends entirely on how it is used. The rebel heart is just as important as the warrior spirit and the two frequently go hand in hand together.

I would go further and say that the rebel heart is vital to facilitate positive change. Without the rebel heart, abusers would never be challenged, dictators would never be toppled and corrupt governments and organisations would continue to rule supreme. In such situations we need a certain amount of rebellion, for it is the catalyst to freedom. Yes, rebellion can be messy and sacrifices have to be made—but on the other side of it usually lies peace and freedom, so it is a battle worth fighting.

Robert the Bruce believed so strongly that his men would follow wherever his heart led them, that he gave orders for his heart to be cut from his body upon his death and carried in a casket to the Holy Land, where his men were to fight on Crusade without him. His heart and his body are buried in two separate places in Scotland, his body in Dunfermline and his heart in Melrose. This is the reason he is known as the original brave heart.

## Rouse the Rebel Heart Spell

You can nurture you own rebel heart to increase your courage and to help you stand up to people who try to bully you, control you or renege on agreements. Simply take a symbol of a heart – this could be a pendent, crystal, stone or a heart cut from card, and hold it to your own heart, saying the following incantation:

⌘

*With warrior spirit I play my part*

*I nurture within my rebel heart*

*I won't be controlled*

*I was born to be free*

*My rebellious heart*
*they now shall see!*

# Mary Queen of Scots – The Captive Queen

One of Scotland's most romantic figures, Mary Queen of Scots, a direct descendent of Robert I and Marjorie Bruce, was the disputed successor to the English throne, plotting against Elizabeth I. Born in Stirling in 1542, she spent her early years in Scotland, before being betrothed to the Dauphin of France and moving to the French court. She was the Queen of France from 1559, until her husband's death in 1560, when she returned to Scotland to take up her rule there, but she was plagued by rebellious Scots who would not be ruled by a woman. This is ironic, to say the least, coming from a region in which Queen Scáthach once trained male warriors!

In 1568, Mary made the mistake of fleeing to England, seeking shelter and support against her Scots enemies. Instead she was imprisoned as a '*royal guest*' of Elizabeth I. Mary was moved from one English castle to another to ensure that no rescue attempt was ever successful. All in all, she spent over eighteen years in captivity. In 1586 she became embroiled in the infamous Babington Plot to assassinate Queen Elizabeth and take the English throne, and for this she was finally executed. She was beheaded for treason at Fotheringhay Castle in 1587.

For all her romance, Mary is also a rather tragic figure, for she was largely used as a pawn in the political intrigues of powerful men. Married three times and crowned twice, yet it could be argued that she never knew a day of security or real autonomy in her life. She is a cautionary tale of why it is so important to know one's own limits and not to over-reach.

## Spell to Know Your Limits

You will need a tea-light and holder for this simple spell. Hold the tea-light in your hands and repeat the incantation three times, then light it in the holder and allow it to burn down. Use this spell whenever you feel tempted to be reckless or to take unnecessary risks.

⌘

*Over-zealous I will not be*

*No captive to my schemes*

*I will not over-reach my plans*

*I know the limit to my dreams!*

# Celtic Meditation:
## The Good King

*You find yourself standing on a castle esplanade where the cobbled street winds its way up to the castle. It is dusk and burning torches are set into the castle walls, making the yellow ochre stone glow golden in the firelight and the cobblestones beneath your feet gleam with a recent rainfall. The torches light your way as you start to walk up the winding road, towards the castle entrance. You pass a sign hung on the wall that says Castle Wynd and nod in silent agreement – it is certainly a winding path, one that takes you ever higher. You trudge on.*

*Eventually you reach the portcullis, which is still drawn up. There are guards standing sentry and holding pikes, but they do not halt your progress. They nod respectfully as you pass. It is almost as if they know you, as if they are expecting you. Passing beneath the portcullis you move into the courtyard. Great braziers are burning, the dancing flames darting and jumping in the autumn breeze. Here you can see many horses and riders, some mounting up and leaving the castle, others returning and handing the reins of their horses on to their young squires. It is a hive of activity, and you make your way through the crowds of people and horses, until you come to the main door of the castle. It's a huge piece of timber, with a pointed arch at the top and a grill in the wood so that strangers can be seen before admittance. Tonight however, the door stands open, ready to receive you and you walk into the castle with a sigh of relief. It is good to be out of the crowds and away from the hustle and bustle of castle life.*

*You look around and find yourself in the Great Hall of the castle. There is a huge fire burning at one end of the hall and you make your way across, eager to feel the heat and warm your hands at the blaze. The pine logs that are burning give off a woodland scent, while the peat that surrounds them smells earthy and rich. You hear footsteps on the rushes behind you and turning you notice a steward, dressed in royal livery, coming towards you. He carries a tray on which is a steaming flagon and a goblet. He bows when he reaches you. "Good evening, Seeker, would you care for some refreshment?" The idea of something warming to drink makes your insides gurgle in anticipation and you smile your thanks. "I would, yes please." The steward pours a goblet of warm red wine and hands it to you. You take a sip and notice it is rich with spices designed to warm you and offer comfort on a cold night. You wrap your hands around the goblet to savour its warmth and watch the steward as he places the tray on a nearby trestle table. "The king will see you now, if you will follow me."*

*But of course! This is why you are here – to seek an audience with the Good King and receive his wise counsel. Eagerly you follow the steward across the Great Hall and into another chamber. There are maps hung on the walls and a great table stands in the centre with yet more maps, with small wooden soldiers and horses placed upon them. This then must be the king's campaign room, where he strategizes his next battle and political manoeuvres.*

*"Sire, the Seeker is here." The steward speaks to someone you hadn't noticed before. A man sits by a much smaller fireplace, gazing into the flames as if lost in thought. He is dressed in fine*

*clothing and wears a cape that looks like it might have been a brown bear once upon a time, but which now makes raiment for royalty. His dark hair curls slightly at his jawline and upon his head he wears a golden crown, encrusted with bright jewels that glimmer in the firelight. He turns and gives you a kindly smile, holding out his hand to you.*

*"Welcome Seeker!" he says, "Come and sit with me by the fire on this chilly night. My steward will pull up a chair for you." You seat yourself in the chair the steward offers and sit for a moment, trying to compose yourself. The Good King assesses you as you sip your spiced wine. "And what can I do for you, Seeker? What need do you have of the man they call the Good King?"*

*"Sire, I have a battle I must face, and I come for your advice."*

*"Ah. And what is the nature of this battle you speak of?"*

*You tell the king of the challenges that you are currently facing, be they small or large, trusting that he will be able to assist you in some way. You know that if anyone can find a way to overcome these challenges it is him. He will know what to do and you put your faith entirely in his guidance.*

*"These are grave concerns, Seeker, and I do not envy you your path. But all paths have bumps in the road at some stage. It is how we navigate those bumps that counts." The king sits in contemplation for a moment, then suddenly he leaps from his chair with the question, "Do you play chess, Seeker?"*

*"Er, a little, sire, though I fear I am a poor player."*

*"Well, we shall see, shall we?"* and the king carries a small table over to the fireplace, upon which is a chess set. He places the table between the two of you and begins to set out the chess pieces. You wonder if he actually heard your concerns at all, or if he simply does not understand the magnitude of the challenges you face. *"You go first, Seeker, I insist."* You move one of the pawns to set the game in motion. For a time, the two of you play in silence, then the king says, *"Have you come up with a strategy?"* You shrug apologetically and reply, *"No sire, my chess isn't that advanced, I'm afraid."*

*"Not for the game, but for the challenge? Do you have a strategy to overcome this battle you face?"*

*"No sire, that is why I'm here. I would ask your advice on it."*

*"My advice? Whatever you do,* ***don't*** *lose your temper! It can lead to a heavy weight resting upon your conscience for the rest of your days. Aye, I wish someone had told* ***me*** *that years ago, when I was young and hot-headed."* He bows his head in a moment of sorrow and reflection. You say nothing. You know of what he speaks, but you cannot help him. *"There is no changing the past,"* he mumbles, *"only learning from it."* He moves another chess piece as he speaks.

*"Sire, I came here because you are a great king and ruler. You must have some direction to give me, for if not, I don't know what I will do. I must win this battle. Everything rests upon it, so I* ***must*** *win, you see."*

*"I do see, Seeker, and I am sorry this issue weighs so heavily upon your heart. However, the fact that so much depends on you winning*

*is exactly what will lead you to victory. Men fight poorly who have no vested interest in the outcome, but if the battle is personal, if there is a vested interest, then victory is much easier to attain. The rest is all in the timing and focus."*

*"Timing and focus? How do you mean?"*

*"I mean simply this – if you think too far ahead, the challenge becomes overwhelming, and defeat is the likely outcome. But if you do not think far enough ahead, then you cannot anticipate your enemy and again defeat is the likely outcome. For victory to unfold, you must think just far enough ahead to make achievable plans and adapt your manoeuvres, but not so far as to become overwhelmed and rigid in the approach. So it really is all in the timing and focus."*

*"I see. But what if the timing is out of my control?"*

*"Then you must work within the parameters of the time that you* **do** *have. Or you stall for more time. The point is, a battle strategy is really just a series of small manoeuvres that are completed in a specific order and sequence. Rather like chess. You make a move, I counter it. I make a move, you counter it. Eventually one of us will win, but it is he who has the wits and the patience to play the long game that is most likely to be victorious. Whatever challenge you face, you need to keep a cool head and be ready to adapt."*

*"Yes, that makes sense. But I wish I had your courage, sire."*

*"Courage! Of course you have courage – you have the Lion Rampant roaring within you! When the hour comes, so will your*

*courage come to the fore, never doubt it. All men quake on the battlefield from time to time. Its natural. But when they must fight, the courage leaps from their heart like a lion! All you need do Seeker, is follow it... Checkmate!" The Good King grins at you as he wins the game and you shake your head, laughing and say, "I told you I was no player."*

*"Better luck next time. Remember I am always here whenever you have need of me, but more than that – know that I reside in your heart, Seeker, always. I am with you in* **every** *battle and challenge you face. You do not go into battle alone, for I am there to guide your steps. When you follow the courage of your own heart, then you follow in my footsteps, then you tread the path of the Good King. Know that I am proud of all your victories and this next one will be no different."*

*"Thank you for your wisdom and guidance, sire. I will remember your words and carry them with me, in my heart."*

*The Good King stands and grasps your forearm in a soldier's handshake. "Blood of my blood, bone of my bone, I give you strength to carry you through, I shine the light which guides you home." He claps you on the back and presses something into your hand. "This will take you back to your own realm, Seeker, but remember I am here if you need me again. Now go forth bravely and with valour." You look down at your hand to see that he has given you a chess piece from the board. It is the king, and with a whoosh, it pulls you down, down, down, away from the castle chamber and back into your waking life.*

## Chapter Five
# Warrior Poets

For the Celts, war was a way of life. They fought to hold territory; they had skirmishes in Clan disputes and they battled for the greater wealth and provision of their people. Battle was as much a part of the Celtic lifestyle as tilling the fields or raising a flock of sheep. Young men had to be battle ready at all times, in case the Clan Chief or local Laird called them to arms. The women needed to be ready to tend wounds and lay out the fallen. Even the children would have been expected to help out, as squires, drummers or water bearers. War was in their DNA.

But the Celts were far more than just petty scrappers or freedom fighters. They were warrior poets. This is a term coined in Scottish and Irish folklore. Put simply, it refers to one who fights for a higher purpose or for a greater good. Warrior poets were idealistic soldiers who fought with a strong moral compass. The idea of committing war crimes would be abhorrent to them, likewise the '*raising of the red dragon*' (not to be confused with the Welsh flag!) which was a banner from Mediaeval times meaning that no mercy would be shown and all enemy forces on the battlefield would be slaughtered, whether they tried to surrender or not. Edward I raised the red dragon against the Scots more than once, so determined was he to crush them. It didn't work, as you will see later in this chapter.

A warrior poet fought with mind, body and spirit. He was a holistic soldier. Brutal force wasn't all that made up a Celtic warrior. In addition to battle skills, he would have developed a strategic mind and he would have held in his heart the reason he was fighting, be that for his Clan, his country or his honour. Honour was hugely important among the Celts. They gave their word and kept it, considering any double dealing or deceit to be cowardly and a sign of weakness.

The warrior poet was motivated by love and compassion, not glory or brutality. If battle came he would face it with courage, but he didn't go out looking for trouble. He would fight to protect his own, considering it an honour to protect his Clan and his loved ones. He was an intelligent warrior, as well as an instinctive one.

In later years, the warrior poets began to document their thoughts and deeds on the battlefield. This gave rise to what we now term The War Poets and much of what we know of the trenches of the first and second world wars, derives from the words written by the warrior poets of the time. This is just one of the ways in which Celtic culture is still prevalent in modern history.

## Becoming a Warrior Poet

We all face troubles from time to time and occasionally we might need to fight our own corner and do battle to defend our rights. Too often though, we go in with a knee-jerk reaction, when we should take a breath and make a calculated response instead. This difference between an unfettered temper tantrum and a more considered response, is what separates a bully from a warrior.

Warriors need not shout, while bullies are full of bravado. Warriors have the ability to control their aggression, while bullies are fuelled by their temper and have little to no control. Warriors know when to attack, mediate, negotiate, placate or fall back. Bullies only know how to attack. Warriors will defend those weaker than themselves, while a bully will target them.

So how do you become more of a warrior poet in your own life? First, take full responsibility for your thoughts, words and deeds. If you make a mistake, own up to it. You're only human and mistakes are allowed. Don't participate in gossip or bullying of any kind – in fact, stand against it, calmly. Be kind. Be helpful to those who might need a hand. Be considerate and show compassion to others.

If someone attacks you in some way, be it a bullying boss or a catty colleague, stand up to them. Literally. Stand up, speak firmly without raising your voice and tell them that you won't be treated that way. What we allow, we condone and we *teach* people how they can treat us. This means that you should never put up with ill-treatment, bullying or controlling behaviour from anyone. Regain your autonomy by standing up for yourself. In this way you will develop the strength of character to face adversity when it comes your way.

Finally, if you do find yourself in a conflict of some kind, breathe deeply before you make your response. Give yourself time to think and to calculate the risks. Then say your piece calmly and firmly, and simply walk away, leaving them to digest your response. If you have done a good job, there should be no need for further engagement. Sadly, conflict is a fact of life. Inevitably you will experience it at some point. When you do, approach it as a warrior poet, with a strong moral compass and compassion for your enemy and you won't go far wrong.

## The Gall-Gaidheal and the Gallowglass

When the Vikings invaded the Celtic regions, they quickly assimilated into the indigenous tribes by marrying native women. Often, they would slaughter the local men at the time of invasion, leaving the way clear for them to have their pick of the womenfolk. One can only imagine how distressing this must have been for the women and children!

However, the result of this enforced breeding and assimilation was an ethnic group of people who were neither strictly Celt nor Norse, but a mixture of both. These were known as the Gall-Gaidheal. This name comes from Gall, meaning stranger or foreigner, so they were the *foreign Gaels*. They were the original outlanders. Over time the Gall-Gaidheal became a respected part of the Celtic community, merging their Norse heritage into Celtic culture and tradition. We still see this influence in parts of the Highlands of Scotland, Ireland, Yorkshire and Lincolnshire, where old Norse words can be seen in some of the place names in those regions.

While the Gall-Gaidheal were happy to settle in one place and make a living from farming, crofting and trade, there were some among them who craved a more adventurous lifestyle. These men were called the Gallowglass, meaning a foreign soldier. They were

seafaring warriors who would travel as mercenaries in the service of their Chief or King and were sometimes called the *sons of death* due to their skill on the battlefield. The Gallowglass played a key role in warfare during the 13th and 14th centuries, and they were extremely active in Scotland and Ireland, under the service of both Robert the Bruce, King of Scots and his brother Edward, who became king of Ireland.

The heritage of the Gall-Gaidheal and the Gallowglass is still evident today with some Scottish and Irish Clans claiming direct descent from these formidable warriors. Clans such as MacDonald, McDougall, MacLeod, MacNeil, Lamont and others, can all claim the Gall-Gaidheal and Gallowglass warriors as their ancient ancestors. In this sense, the Gall-Gaidheal still walk among us today, so they are far from gone and are very much a part of modern society.

## Creating a Battle Plan for Life

The Celts were great strategists. They knew exactly what they wanted from any conflict or negotiation. Holding the end point in mind is essential in any victory, because otherwise how will you know when you have won? You don't want to go on fighting, way past the point where you had exactly what you were fighting for, because that way you will only exhaust yourself. You must know exactly what victory or success looks like to you, so that you can recognise when you have reached that point and take a well-earned break.

This is as true for life as it is for warfare. The truth is that life will feel like less of a battleground if you approach it with a strategy in place. Those people who drift through life with no goals, no ambitions and no direction are usually the ones who end up most dissatisfied, unfulfilled, miserable and envious of others.

Take charge of your future by formulating a strategic battle plan. This will help you to keep on track with your goals and get you to where you want to be. Achievement is an important life-skill to master because it leads to greater personal confidence. The more confidence you have the more open you will be to new experiences and opportunities. Once you have ticked off most of your goals, make a new battle plan to keep your life moving forward.

## The Battle Plan

Take a large sheet of paper and divide it into three equal sections, like so:

Short Term Goals – 0–6 months:

Mid-Term Goals – 6 months–2 years:

Long Term Goals – 2–5years:

Next, begin to fill out each section. List all the things that you want to achieve in the next six months. Make sure these goals are realistic for the time frame you are working with. If they're not achievable in six months, put them in one of the other sections. Try to have a mixture of personal, career and hobby goals so that you are improving your life-balance as you go. Once you have filled out the first section, move onto the next two sections. When you have your battle plan all figured out, you effectively have the next five years of your life mapped out on paper. Each time you achieve a goal, tick it off.

Keep your Battle Plan in a safe place, perhaps on your altar. Once you have written it all out, roll it up like a scroll and bless it by passing it through incense smoke as you say:

⌘

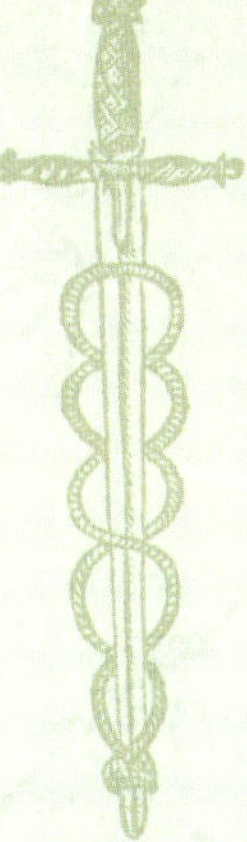

*I feel the need to press ahead*

*To make my dreams come true*

*As I make my goals reality*

*My life is shaped anew*

*I learn from Celtic Ancestors*

*To hold my battle ground*

*I create my own sense of victory*

*To my own success I'm bound.*

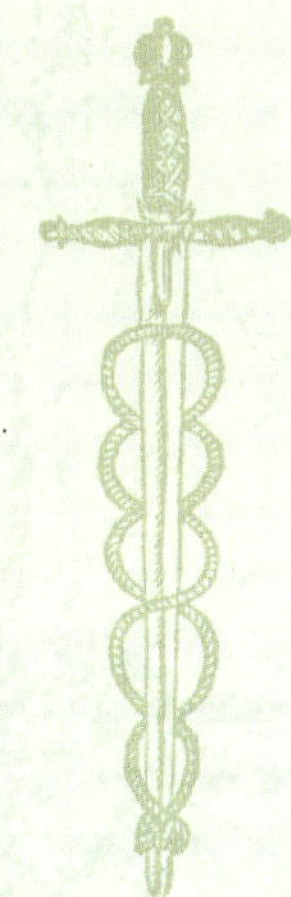

## NOTABLE WARRIOR POETS

⌘ **Sir William Wallace**–quite possibly the most famous Celtic freedom fighter in the UK, if not the world, Wallace successfully routed the much larger army of Edward I at the Battle of Stirling Bridge in 1297. He stirred up the Scots to stand against the oppression of English occupation, until he was betrayed and captured by Sir John Menteith and taken to London, where he was executed in 1305. He is still Scotland's national hero and a global icon for freedom and independence.

⌘ **Isabella MacDuff, Countess of Buchan** – Isabella is a great heroine of Scotland because she defied her Comyn husband and rode out to crown his rival, Robert the Bruce, King of Scots! This was an ancient right of the Earls of Fife, but with her brother, who was Earl at that time, imprisoned in England, Isabella took it upon herself to honour this tradition. For her boldness and bravery, she was harshly punished, being confined to live in a cage hung on the outside of Berwick castle.

⌘ **Rob Roy Macgregor** – Rob Roy was a Jacobite who fought in support of the exiled Stuart King James. He was known for both protecting and raiding cattle, for which he was branded an outlaw. He fought at the Jacobite Uprising of 1715 and died in 1734. He is buried at Balquidder, near his home on Loch Lomond, with his wife Mary and two of their sons. He will always be known as a Child of the Mists and Macgregor Despite Them.

- ⌘ **Llywelyn ap Gruffudd** – Son of Llywelyn the Great, Llywelyn ap Gruffudd is known as the Last Prince of Wales, from 1258–1282. That is, he was the very last sovereign and Welsh born Prince of Wales. Llywelyn refused to pay homage to King Edward I and was a key figure in the rebellion against him. He was therefore declared a rebel, much like William Wallace. His family were allies of Clan Comyn in the Highlands of Scotland. Upon Llywelyn's death, Edward named his son, the future Edward II, Prince of Wales, as a symbol of his conquest of Wales.

## Toasting the Water

Toasting the water is a common practice in Scotland and it can easily be incorporated into your magical rituals. Simply pass the ritual chalice of wine, or a glass of whisky as is more traditional, over a jug or cauldron of water and make a toast or a wish before drinking.

This tradition is associated with the Jacobites, the supporters of the Stuart Kings in the 18th Century, of which Rob Roy was one and he would have indulged in this tradition himself. To keep their support a secret, they would silently toast their leader, who was in exile across the water in France. This was a good way for Jacobites to show their allegiance and to recognise one another. It is said that the practice has its origins in ancient Pictish magic, but it is still performed today by Scots all over the world, as a toast to their ancestral roots. Before you drink say "*Slainte mhath!*" which is a Gaelic toast to good health.

## Brave Heart Spell for Adventure

If you ever feel trapped, caged or hemmed in, this spell can help you to take back your autonomy and rouse your spirit of adventure! Take a golden candle for new opportunities and carve the words Brave Heart and Adventure down the length of it. Light the candle and chant the incantation three times, then let the candle burn down:

⌘

*Razzle, dazzle flying free*

*The spirit of adventure carries me*

*From a mundane cage I now depart*

*I unleash my power as a true brave heart!*

## Ghostly Warrior Poets

With so many battles and skirmishes throughout their bloody history, it should come as no surprise that the Celtic regions are said to be populated with many ghosts and hauntings. Whether these are echoes of the past that occasionally bleed through into our own time, or the restless spirits of ancient warrior poets, I'll leave you to decide for yourself, but one thing is clear – Celtic folklore is full of ghostly tales. Here are just a few of them to whet your appetite.

## The Dunoon Massacre

The coastal town of Dunoon, on the Cowal peninsular of Argyll, was ruled by Clan Lamont, who were descended from the Irish Clan O'Neill. Their seat was Toward Castle, which stood proudly on the coastline, overlooking the Firth of Clyde. The ruins of the castle still stand today, and they are said to be haunted by various members of Clan Lamont who were murdered during the Dunoon Massacre in 1646. The massacre came about because the Lamont's neighbours, Clan Campbell, had been disputing the rightful ownership of land. Basically, they were making a land grab on Lamont territory to further enrich their own Clan. While the Campbells were away fighting at the Battle of Inverlochy, some of the Lamonts stayed behind and managed to lay waste some of Campbell territory in reprisal. Afterwards, it seemed as if the Campbells had learnt their lesson and the dispute had been settled, but the following summer the Campbells requested hospitality from their neighbours, and by the laws of honourable conduct in the Highlands, the Lamonts couldn't refuse. So, the Campbells marched into Toward Castle, feasted and drank with the Lamonts and then retired for the night as honoured guests. However, as soon as the whole castle lay sleeping, the Campbells stealthily rose from their chambers and set about killing their hosts in their beds! This was a huge violation of the hospitality tradition and a bitter betrayal of the Lamonts' trust. More than two hundred men, women and children were murdered in the massacre at the hands of the Campbells. Their ghosts are said to walk the ruins of Toward Castle at night, forever bemoaning the betrayal of Highland hospitality. Who can blame them?

## The Great Massacre of Glencoe

Glencoe in the Highlands of Scotland is an area of such outstanding natural beauty; it really has to be seen to be believed. It is a place that should be *experienced*, rather than simply admired from afar. The mountains, majestic and glowering, tower over the deep glen and the River Coe. It is a place where many a climber and hillwalker has been caught out by the sudden change in weather conditions, turning a pleasant hike into a battle for survival. Make no mistake about it, the landscape of Glencoe is as brutal

as it is beautiful. It is a powerful place, but quite apart from the foreboding hills, there is an atmosphere of sorrow, for it is here in this beautiful glen, the ancestral home of Clan MacDonald, that the Great Massacre of Glencoe took place in deep winter in 1692. At that time, King William III (William of Orange) was on the throne and he wanted to be sure that he stamped out any notion of Jacobite rebellion, so he ordered that all subjects, including the Chiefs of Clans known to be Jacobite supporters, should swear allegiance to him, or face reprisal.

In sleepy Glencoe, the chief of Clan Macdonald realised that he would have to swear the oath of allegiance to the new king, even though he and his Clan were Jacobites. Better to swear the oath and live to fight another day, than to be executed or imprisoned before he and his Clan could raise a sword in a future Jacobite uprising. So he set off through the snow to swear his oath, but he arrived late and was then considered to have defaulted. In reprisal, government forces, led by the Campbells (yes, them again!) were sent out to MacDonald lands in Glencoe to seek hospitality and respite from the bitterly cold weather. Can you see where this is going? Of course, as Highland honour dictated, the MacDonalds welcomed their guests – and of course, they paid the price for it as hospitality was once again betrayed by the Campbells and they murdered the MacDonalds in their beds.

The intention was to make an example of The MacDonalds as a warning to *all* Jacobites. Some of the MacDonalds fled, but the snowy conditions of Glencoe in mid-February meant that many of those who escaped the sword simply froze to death on the mountains instead. Their spirits are said to haunt the misty region of Glencoe, where they are believed to help unwary travellers find their way to safety when lost in the hills of their ancestral homelands, flitting in and out of the mist as guides, though who knows what these ghosts would do if they were to come face to face with a modern-day Campbell?! Today there is a visitor centre in the heart of Glencoe which commemorates the MacDonalds. Here they exhibit items that relate the tragedy of the Massacre, including the very chilling letter that ordered the political murder of the Clan MacDonald.

## Culloden Moor

Culloden Moor, near Inverness in the Scottish Highlands is regarded as Britain's largest war grave, where approximately 1500 soldiers are buried, though, sadly, it is not yet protected by law from property developers. It is on this field that the Jacobites made what was to be their last stand against English Government forces in April 1746. Thousands of men were killed in the battle, mostly Scotsmen and Jacobites who were vastly outnumbered and under-equipped. They fought the Highland way, predominantly with swords, dirks and targes, while the Government forces had cannon, muskets and bayonets. While some Jacobites also had access to firearms and artillery weapons, they were outgunned by the opposition. After just an hour or so of battle, the Red Coats of the Government Forces had won. Now all that was left to do was clear the battlefield, which became a mass grave. Culloden Moor is dotted throughout with small standing stones, each marking the graves of a particular Clan. It is a very sad and atmospheric place to visit, but more than that, it is said to be one of the most haunted sites in Scotland. One particular spirit cannot seem to get over his disappointment at the outcome of the battle and the war. He can sometimes be seen wandering the battlefield, looking grief-stricken as he shakes his head and cries *"Defeated! Defeated! All is lost!"* On other occasions ghostly Jacobites have been seen charging across the moor, weapons raised, still ready to meet the enemy who defeated them centuries ago. Defeated they might have been in history, but not in death it seems, for these warrior poets still fight on.

## Monks of Conwy Castle

Conwy Castle in North Wales was built by Edward I as a way of declaring his power to the Welsh. It is one of the most impressive Mediaeval castles in the British Isles, with much of it still standing, including the Royal Apartments. It was a symbol of strength and of the subjugation of the Welsh people by the English king, who went on to declare his own son the new Prince of Wales, later to become Edward II. However, it seems that some former residents were not in favour of the new order of power. Legend states that the castle was built on the site of an old Welsh monastery and as a result, ghostly monks can be seen wandering around the castle in their robes and occasionally the haunting sound of religious chanting can be heard. Perhaps that is why King Edward and his son rarely stayed at Conwy!

# Celtic Meditation: **The Sword of Freedom**

*You find yourself standing in the heart of Ettrick Forest, the trees growing thickly all around. In the distance you can just make out a couple of doe deer, calmly munching on the shrubs and roots, their scut-tails flicking back and forth. You watch them for a moment, mesmerised by their delicate charm. Suddenly you hear a sound whizz by your ear and an arrow lodges itself into the tree that stands directly in front of you. You duck instinctively, your hands shielding your head in protection. With a stealthy motion, a giant comes towards you. No, not a giant, a man – but he must be well over six feet tall. He wears leather armour and a tunic, over trews that cover his legs, protecting them from the barbs of thistles and helping to camouflage him in the forest. His hair is long, matching his impressive beard for thickness. You can see the hilt of a mighty sword protruding over his shoulder, from where it is slung across his back, so immense is its size.*

*"Let that be a warning to you, Seeker. Never let your guard down!" The huge man offers you his hand and helps you up off the floor. "Thank you," you say, then more indignantly, "You almost hit me!" The man throws back his head and laughs as he claps you on the shoulder warmly. "If I'd meant to hit you, Seeker, you'd be dead now! Don't you know who I am?"*

*You take in the height of the man, his skill with a bow and the massive sword he wears, and you nod your head, saying, "I know you. You're Sir William Wallace."*

*"Aye, that's me. And what brings you to Ettrick Forest, Seeker?" You find yourself telling Wallace all about the struggles you are enduring, the enemies you face and the life issues that are grinding you down. You leave nothing out, pouring your heart out to the man whose name would be imprinted on history for his courage and fortitude for centuries to come. Remembering how his life was to end, you bow your head for a moment in honour of this great warrior, but you do not, cannot, speak of it. Instead, you ask, "How do you keep going? I find it so hard to just face each day right now. I truly don't know how you do what you do."*

*"What other choice do we have, Seeker, but to keep pressing on and moving forward? The world will not stop just because we do. It will move on without us. It will leave you behind and you will find it more difficult than ever to catch up with yourself again, with your hopes and dreams and ambitions. If you give up, all is lost. The way I see it, our only option is to be up and doing."*

*"But* ***why*** *do you fight, Sir William? What keeps that sword tied to your back and in your hand? Why do you not lay down your arms and accept that change must come?"*

*"I fight because they took all that I held dear, and I will never have it back again. But I will not let them take my country, my freedom, my voice of opposition. I will fight for as long as I can hold a sword. And then, my name will fight on in the pages of history, long after I'm gone. You know that this is true, Seeker." Your head snaps up as he says this, and you notice his eyes narrow as he fixes you with his gaze. "Aye – I know what's coming to me. But I also know that*

***my*** *end is not* **the** *end. It's really just the beginning. I'm a catalyst for change. You can be too, in your own life."*

*"But how? I have no skills to fight with, I'm not a warrior like you."*

*"It's true the fight you face is different and it requires different skills, but it still requires the same fortitude, Seeker, and you* **do** *have fortitude. You just have to dig deep enough to find it." The two of you remain silent for a time, watching the deer, then Wallace says, "You think that all is lost, Seeker, when the truth is, you still have everything to play for, to fight for – aye, and to win, too! History* **embellishes** *the truth, but victories do not come with a fanfare. They come thorough blood, sweat and tears. They come when you are knee-deep in mud and in the bodies of those who have fallen by the wayside. Sometimes, victory comes so silently, you barely notice it, but it's there, hidden in the fabric of your life. One thing I do know for certain, though."*

*"What's that?" you ask.*

*"You have to be up and doing to get anywhere. If you give up, or give in, then you've lost already, and the battle will be fought by another." He removes his great sword from its place on his back and stands it point down towards the ground, his big hands wrapped around the hilt. "Come Seeker and take the strength you need from me and my sword. Together we have fought many, many battles, some lost, some won despite the odds beings stacked against us. But always, we fought on, my sword and I, a force to be reckoned with! Come, place your hands on the hilt, right by mine." You do as Wallace instructs and place your hands alongside his, on the hilt*

*of what was to become known as the Sword of Freedom. "You feel that?" he asks, and you nod your head in wonder at the vibration of the sword beneath your hands. "That is strength, Seeker. It is fortitude, courage and victory. Take it with you back to your own realm and use it well. When life gets hard, think of* **me***. Remember that I am always here if you have need of me again."*

*You turn to walk out of the forest but then stop. You* **have** *to say something. You feel that you* **must** *warn him of what is to be, so you turn and say, "Sir William! Be careful who you trust.* **Please***, be careful who you trust."*

*Wallace steps forward, his sword planted between his feet and held firmly in his hands. "I know what is to come, Seeker. Have neither fear nor sorrow for me, for I have the courage to be the catalyst." There is the shine of tears in his eyes as he speaks. You say your farewells, then you turn and walk away from Sir William Wallace, away from the Sword of Freedom, taking their mighty strength with you, out of the forest and down, down, down, back into your waking life.*

## Chapter Six

# The Otherworld

**Celtic culture is full of superstition and folklore, which should come as no surprise given that the Celts are a storytelling community. While many of their folkloric beings were originally thought to be a benevolent force, with the rise of Christianity came the demonization of the Celtic fey. As you will see, many of these folkloric spirits are now linked with death or are considered to be bad omens, yet originally they were simply messengers from the Otherworld, with magical powers and gifts to share with those who were fortunate enough to see them. Do bear this in mind as you read about these magical beings.**

## The Cailleach – Blue Hag of Winter

The Cailleach is the Celtic goddess of winter. She is occasionally depicted as a seductive young ice-maiden, but more usually as an old woman with blue tinged skin. She brings the cold season and sprinkles the mountains with snow. She makes the world over with frost, ice and snowflakes. The Cailleach wants people to enjoy the gifts of her season, to enjoy a cold, frosty walk or skiing in the mountains, before returning home to a warm hearthside and a hearty bowl of soup. She protects those who welcome her and her season, but she can be something of a trickster to those who moan about the winter weather, causing slips and falls and all manner of winter problems.

As a spirit of winter, she should be welcomed at the time of the autumnal equinox or Samhain at the latest, with the house made ready for the colder months to come. Preparing for the winter is a good way to honour this deity and to keep on her good side as it shows a healthy, mindful respect for the cold weather, so feel free to light a winter-scented candle in honour of the Cailleach as you go about hanging warmer curtains, laying down thick rugs or even chopping wood for the wood-burner if you have one. Fill up the freezer with goodies, stock up on candles and buy any new winter clothes you need. Make sure your winter sports gear, such as ice skates, are in good condition and see to any repairs that need doing before the dark of winter really sets in. The Cailleach will appreciate all such preparations for her season.

In Scotland they say "*The Cailleach is on you*" if someone is suffering from the effects of the cold and showing signs of hyperthermia. Their skin will take on a blue tinge, just like the Blue Hag herself, and they will feel numb and very sleepy, showing symptoms of extreme shivering and teeth chattering as they begin to warm up. When the Cailleach is on you, heed her warning and retreat indoors, take a tot of whisky in a hot drink and allow yourself to warm up gradually, by a warm fireside.

The Cailleach isn't malevolent. She is simply winter and she must be respected as such, for winter can be a dangerous time. Enjoy her season, but ere on the side of caution by casting this spell for her protection before you venture out into the cold for any length of time.

## CAILLEACH SPELL FOR A SAFE WINTER

You will need a blue-lace agate crystal, or a token that represents the winter time, such as a snowflake brooch or necklace. On the night when the clocks go back and British summer time ends, or a dark night in your time zone, light a tea light and place it into a lantern. Take this outside, along with your winter token and sit for moment, breathing in the dark, autumnal air. Know that from now on the days will become visibly shorter and the nights longer, colder and darker. Hold your winter token in your hands, look up at the sky and say:

⌘

*I welcome the Cailleach, I welcome the Blue Hag*

*I ask her protection as the sky rains black*

*I call on the Cailleach to watch over us all*

*To see us through winter and every snowfall*

*I honour the Cailleach with this glowing flame*

*I welcome the winter in her name*

*As I enjoy all her gifts of winter's delight*

*I ask her protection, from now till Spring's light.*

*Protecting us all with warmth, wealth and good cheer*

*As we feast with our family, throughout the next year!*

*So mote it be.*

Leave the lantern outside until the tea-light has burnt itself out. Put the crystal or token into your winter coat pocket, or wear it, so that you carry it with you throughout the winter months. If you want, you can cast this spell with several crystals or tokens, one for each family member, to keep them safe through the snowy season of winter.

## Washer at the Ford

The Washer, or *ban nighe*, is another form of Hag spirit and is thought by some to be an aspect of the Cailleach. Similar to the *ban sidhe* or banshee, to see the Washer at the Ford is an omen, even if it is only in a dream. She appears at the side of a loch or stream, washing a plaid. If the plaid is washed clean, it was a good omen, but if she washed blood from the plaid and the water turned red, it was a sign that someone close would die. The colours of the plaid were also significant, as this would foretell which Clan the omen referred to. If she was washing sheets stained with blood, this meant a death in childbirth, be it mother or babe. Originally, the Washer at the Ford would grant three wishes to those who saw her and spoke to her unafraid, but the rise of Christianity dissolved this aspect of the superstition and made the Washer a harbinger of death. In her aspect as a water spirit, her role was to guard the water she was linked to, and libations of whisky, cider or beer would be poured into the water to keep this spirit benevolent and ward off her bad omens.

# The Spaewife

A *spaewife* is a woman who has the gift of healing and psychic ability, sometimes known as *second sight* or *the sight*. She is often associated with magic and witchcraft and she was a valued member of the Clan, up until the time when the witch hunts gripped Britain and Europe, when anyone thought to be a spaewife would most likely have been accused of witchcraft and executed accordingly, particularly during the reign of James VI of Scotland, who later became James I of England too and who was relentless in his pursuit of so-called witches.

The term comes from the old Norse word *spa*, which meant prophecy. This word was amalgamated with the old Scots language to become *spae*, hence *spaewife*. In some legends the spaewife is a fairy woman or one who has fairy ancestry. To marry such a woman was considered very lucky, as she would bring her husband good fortune and abundance with her fey magic.

The *selkie wife* is another version of the spaewife, being a seal who can transform into a woman. Folklore says that when the selkies come ashore to dance, they cast off their seal skins and dance skyclad, or naked, on the beach. If a man should find a selkie's seal skin and hide it, she has no choice but to become his wife. Then he would enjoy rich harvests and an abundant catch whenever he went out to sea, but if the selkie wife ever found her seal skin, she would immediately return to the ocean in her seal form and her husband would never see her again.

## The Tylwyth Teg

In Welsh folklore the Tylwyth Teg are a type of fairy folk who reside in the court of Gwyn Ap Nudd. They are said to be drawn to small children, especially those with golden hair, and they will steal children away if they get the chance, leaving a changeling in their place. However, they will also watch over and protect mortal children too, providing they are well dressed and live in a clean and tidy house! The Tylwyth Teg can't abide disorder, and they will punish slovenliness by playing tricks on the lazy housekeeper. However, they will also reward an industrious housewife with the gift of a silver coin left on the hearth, which is as good a reason as any to do the housework!

## The Wild Hunt

Probably one of the spookiest aspects of Celtic folklore, The Wild Hunt is well known in various mythologies, including Scottish, Irish, Welsh and Norse. As the name suggests, the Wild Hunt is a hunting party, but one that you would not wish to saddle up for! It is a spectral Hunt, led by a phantom Horseman, with a pack of ghostly hounds running alongside his midnight black mount. Legend states that both horse and hounds have glowing red eyes and foaming mouths, while the Horseman is hooded – or headless!

To see or hear the Wild Hunt has long been considered to be a bad omen and although it can be encountered at any time of year, it is more usual for this legend to resurface during the dark autumn and winter months. The Wild Hunt rides in on the billowing clouds of a storm filled sky. The eerie sound of the hunting horn blows in on the wind, trumpeting through the treetops. The Wild Hunt's purpose is to gather up the souls of the dead and carry them away to the Otherworld.

The Horseman who leads the Hunt is by turns Arawn, Cernunnos, Herne the Hunter, Gwyn ap Nudd or Odin, depending on the region and culture. In Ireland he is associated with Dullachan, a headless horseman who wanders the byways looking for lost souls to take. Again, the Dullachan, or Dark Man, was said to be a harbinger of death. Even today having '*Dark Man dreams*' or nightmares of shadowy figures, is linked with anxiety, worry, depression, despair and melancholia, so heed this message from your subconscious if you experience such dreams on a regular basis, and seek out the help if you need it.

It is safe to say that Washington Irving was probably inspired by the folklore of the Wild Hunt when he wrote *The Legend of Sleepy Hallow* and the Hunt remains a prevalent aspect of Celtic folklore. While you are unlikely to see the Hunt in full force, you might experience hints of it—in the shapes of storm clouds or the sound of the autumn wind blowing through the forests and hills. It was said that hiding in a kirk or church would protect one from the Hunt as it rode by, but avoid sheltering under yew trees, for they are portals through which the Huntsman rides and you will put yourself directly in his path!

## PROTECTION FROM THE WILD HUNT

To this day, it is still considered to be a very bad omen if you should witness the Wild Hunt, so as it rides through the sky on stormy tides, it is always a good idea to say this simple protective incantation as you hear the storm coming in:

⌘

*Wild Hunt, Storm Rider,*

*Pass by me and mine*

*Leave safe this house, no ill to bear*

*In your wake leave all benign.*

## The Mirrie Dancers

On a much brighter note, the Mirrie Dancers are said to be an omen of *good* fortune and to see them dancing is said to be very lucky indeed. Also known as Fox Fire, Northern Lights or the Aurora Borealis, the Mirrie Dancers have delighted onlookers all over the northern hemisphere. Caused by atmospheric conditions, in the darkest winter nights the sky lights up with swirls of green and blue and golden light. It shimmers and dances through the sky, in a similar motion to the starling murmurations in autumn. I have seen the Mirrie Dancers myself in the Scottish Highlands and it is the most magical experience. If you are lucky enough to see them, be sure to make a wish! As an alternative to travelling, view the Northern Lights online, then say this spell for added good fortune:

⌘

*Mirrie Dancers shining bright*

*Fox Fire, bring your light*

*Fill my life with luck and charm*

*A love who keeps me safe from harm*

*Swirling, dancing through the night*

*Fire of gold and emerald bright*

*No matter where on earth I roam*

*I take with me the light of home.*

# Celtic Meditation:
# A Winter Song of Snowflakes

*You find yourself standing upon the sloping shoulders of Ben Cruachan, in the Grampian Mountains. Looking up you see that the peak of the mountain is lost in the mist high above you. It is a cool autumn day, and the landscape is a riot of bronze and brown and gold, with old heather and ferns displaying their autumn shades. You set off walking up the mountain path, taking careful steps on the rocky terrain. The walk is hard, the gradient steep but instinct pushes you on, ever upwards. You know that you must get to the top of the mountain. You need to see the world from a higher perspective and the summit beckons, drawing you on.*

*You hardly notice when the rain begins to fall in big heavy drops, pattering on the trees and shrubs around you. The mountain is a lonely place. You haven't seen any wildlife at all, not a bird, squirrel or stag has crossed your path, which seems odd, but you put the thought to the back of your mind. You concentrate on your footing as the path narrows to more of a deer track. The rain is heavier now and you can't help but notice that the weather has taken a turn for the worse. Still, your inner drive pushes you onwards up the mountain. It is a tiring climb, and you pause for a moment to catch your breath. The rain has turned the deer track to mud, slick under foot, the path narrowing and becoming more of a rabbit run. On either side, the trees blow fiercely in the wind which is becoming increasingly strong as you make your way up Ben Cruachan, but you tell yourself that this is just because you are climbing higher up the mountain. You trudge on, your head bowed as you lean into the wind and the gradient. You know that you're quite close to the summit now. It can't be much further. You need to press on.*

*The wind takes a sudden shift in direction and hits you with an icy blast of air which takes your breath away. The rain is turning to sleet, then snow and you stop to ponder your options. This clearly isn't the weather for a hike, yet you've already come so far, it seems silly to turn back now, so close to the summit. So you press ahead, as the snowflakes flurry around and gather on your eyelashes and melt into your hair.*

*All at once you hear a tinkling silvery voice on the wind, singing a refrain. "Come Seeker, come hither, the mountain awaits. Come Seeker, come hither, as winter awakes!" It is almost as if the snowflakes themselves are singing to you. You stop for a moment and listen, smiling into the frosty wind, watching the snowflakes as they swirl and dance, blowing back down the mountain. The snow is falling more steadily now and what began as the odd gentle flake soon becomes a mountain blizzard. You cannot see your way ahead, but you drive on through the snow, forwards and upwards, ever higher and higher.*

*As you break out through the treeline and emerge from their sheltering boughs, the wind screams down on you like a Bean Sidhe and you realise now that you're in trouble. The weather is too strong, too powerful. You shouldn't be on the mountain. It feels suddenly very dangerous, and you realise how out of your depth you are as the blizzard shrieks around you.*

*"STOP!" a voice cries, vibrant and echoing across the Grampian Mountains. You freeze in your steps, quite literally, because as you*

*glance down you see that your feet have been rooted to the spot in a cobweb of ice, anchoring you in place. At the same time, the snowflakes settle to the ground, like glitter in a snow-globe, and you begin to see what lies in front of you.*

*You have indeed reached the summit and there in front of you sits a giant of a woman, enthroned upon a crag of black rock. A pure white stag stands quietly beside her, his silver antlers shimmering in the snow-light. The woman's skin has a pale bluish hue, and*

*her face is old and wizened. Her snow-white hair hangs past her shoulders, which are clad in some kind of fur that might once have been a wolf. Across her lap she holds a staff which she now points directly at you. "**Why** do you disobey me, Seeker?"*

*"Disobey you? But I haven't disobeyed you."*

*"You know who I am, I suppose, or must I explain **that** too?"*

*"I know you, lady. You are the Cailleach, the Queen of Winter and one of the Old Ones."*

*"Well, the Seeker knows that much at least," the Cailleach says to the stag beside her, who nods his antlers in amused agreement. "Why have you come here, Seeker? I did not summon you."*

*"I came to find a new perspective. I thought the view from the mountain may help me to see the world differently."*

*"I see. And yet you ignored all my warnings."*

*"Warnings, lady? What warnings?"*

*"First of all, I cleared the mountain to show you that today is not the day for a stroll. Did you see any wildlife, Seeker, any birds, squirrels or stags? No, you did not, for my whispers sent them home to their nests and drays. Secondly, I sent the wind and rain to turn you back down the mountain to safety, yet still you came onwards. Thirdly, I sent the snowflakes to sing out a clear warning to you that the mountain would wait, that it would always be here for you to climb on another day, because today winter is wakeful, restless and dangerous, yet still you did not listen! I sent these messages not to summon you, Seeker, but to send you safe home."*

*"Oh. My apologies, lady, I fear I misunderstood your meaning."*

*"You did indeed," says the Cailleach standing and walking over to you, "Look," she points to a small Scots pine, just beginning to grow at the edge of the treeline, "There is a time for growth, Seeker and a time for rest, a time for adventure and a time for stillness." As she speaks the Cailleach leans down and gently pulls the blanket of snow around the tiny tree, tucking it in and whispering "There my pretty, sleep now. The winter is here. Rest your roots." Then she straightens up and fixes you with her icy gaze, "***Why*** must you always, ***always press ahead***, Seeker?! Why must you always work, achieve and be productive?"*

*You bow your head, shamefaced and say, "I don't know. I suppose I just want to make the most of my life, to prove that I* ***can*** *be a success, that I'm not lazy, or useless, or unworthy. I am driven to keep going, so that no one thinks less of me."*

*"I give you a beautiful winter, one that is cold and frosty and designed to make you slow down, to sleep more, to have fun in the snow so that you can be more grateful for the warm home you have when you go indoors. I give you all this, year after year, so that you may understand the importance of rest, Seeker. Winter is a time of hibernation and cocooning, yet you carry on as if it is still high summer and you are meant to be active at all times. You're not. You're meant to slow down and rest in the wintertime, aye, and for periods of time throughout the year too. That is my gift to you.* ***That*** *is the new perspective that you seek!"*

*"I see. Yes, it makes sense to me now. I know that I do have a tendency to push myself too hard and I will remember the lesson you have taught me." The Cailleach puts her chilly hand on your cheek and says softly, "You are not being lazy, Seeker, when you slow down. You are keeping winter in the way it was meant to be kept. When you hunker down, you honour me. When you sleep by the fireside, you honour me. When you play in the snow, you celebrate my gifts and when you slow down, you live by* ***my*** *schedule, whatever time of year it may be."*

*"I will slow down. I will remember not to push myself too hard. Thank you for your wisdom, Cailleach."*

*"The mountain isn't going anywhere Seeker. You don't need to climb it all in one day! Remember to pace yourself properly, to alter your perspective on rest. Now it is time for you to return to your own realm." The Cailleach pulls something out from behind her rocky throne. It is a small sledge, which she attaches to a harness on the white stag. "Sylvan will take you home. Come, sit." You go over to the sledge and sit comfortable amid the furs, as the Cailleach bids you farewell. You suddenly feel very, very tired. "Your rest starts now, Seeker. Go at a slower pace and life will be much better for you," she steps back and calls, "Take the Seeker home, Sylvan." With a jiggle of bells, the stag pulls the sledge through the snow, and you hear a final call from the Cailleach. "Rest your roots, Seeker! Rest. Your. Roots!" And with that, Sylvan trots on, and the sledge pulls you down Ben Cruachan, down the snowy mountain, down, down, down and back into your waking life.*

I R S

## Chapter Seven

# Heraldic Beasts and Celtic Creatures

Power animals or totems are an important aspect of Celtic magic. The Celts believed in a wide range of fantastical and mythical creatures, a few of which we will be looking at in this chapter. Some of those creatures took on prominent places in Celtic culture, for instance the red dragon in Wales or the unicorn in Scotland. Depicted on flags, shields, targes and carved in stone, animal totems stride through Celtic mythology and history, some even maintaining their place of honour to this day. Working with them in magic is largely an exercise of visualisation, which means that no matter where you are or what you are doing, you always have access to these fabled creatures to give you a magical edge in your daily life.

## The Unicorn

One of the heraldic beasts of Scotland, and still present on the British coat of arms, the pure white unicorn is a symbol of purity, liberty, freedom, chastity and virtue. In 15th and 16th century Scotland, it was a form of currency, with coins called Unicorns and Half-Unicorns in distribution. To this day statues of the unicorn can be seen all over Scotland, from Inverness to Edinburgh, and along with the Red Lion Rampant, the unicorn holds up the Scottish flag in heraldic design.

Magically speaking, the unicorn is associated with the moon. It's spiralled horn, the alicorn, was said to be able to detect poison and purify water. In mythology it could not be held by chains or bars; it gallops so swiftly it could never be caught and was only captured by a maiden – that is a female virgin of virtuous intent. The unicorn is a universal symbol of magic, miracles, enchantment and innocence the world over. Although a gentle creature, it can also be very ferocious when crossed, defending its liberty valiantly. Perhaps this is the reason the Scots took it as one of their heraldic beasts? It is certainly regarded as a very protective totem and one which can inspire you towards greater independence. The unicorn is still known as one of the King's Beasts and is associated with the current British monarchy.

## UNICORN SPELL FOR INDEPENDENCE

Cast this spell whenever you feel your independence and autonomy are being compromised. Take a picture or statue of a unicorn and place it on the altar before you. Place a pure white spiralled candle nearby in a suitable holder and light it. This represents the magical alicorn. Think about the ways in which your independence is being curtailed, then visualise a unicorn galloping towards you to carry you away into a life of greater liberty and freedom. Say this incantation nine times:

⌘

*Sacred horse of equine grace*

*I call your spirit to this place*

*Bring your strength, protection and light*

*For my freedom I will fight*

*None shall take my liberty*

*As I ride with you, wild and free!*

Allow the alicorn candle to burn down and take steps to increase your sense of independence and freedom.

## HOW TO CREATE AN ALICORN WAND

You can enhance your magic by using an alicorn wand. This is a wand that you have fashioned to represent the magical horn of a unicorn. You will need a stick of wood or dowelling, silver paint, silver or white glitter, glue, a white satin ribbon long enough to wrap around the stick, and a pointed aurora borealis crystal.

First paint the stick all over using the silver paint. While the paint is still tacky, roll the wand into silver or white glitter until it shimmers. Once thoroughly dried, glue the crystal to one end to form the wand's tip, then wrap the ribbon clockwise around the wand in a spiral motion to give the wand an ailcorn effect. Glue the ribbon in place as you go, paying particular attention to the ends. Allow the glue to dry, then bless the wand by passing it through incense smoke and saying:

⌘

*Alicorn wand of enchantment and light*

*Shine unicorn magic, bring all that is bright*

*Add to my magic, lend unicorn charm*

*As I use this wand to enchant and disarm.*

Use the alicorn wand to direct energy in your spells, just as you would use any other type of magical wand.

## The Water Kelpie

In Scottish folklore the fearsome water kelpie is a malevolent water spirit that takes on the guise of a beautiful black or grey horse, grazing peacefully by the side of a loch. Its seemingly gentle nature is designed to draw in the unwary, for if one tries to pet the horse, or ride it, it will leap into the depths of the loch and drown its unfortunate rider. In some tales the water kelpie becomes a black unicorn and is an omen of death. It is afraid of iron, being a fairy horse, so carrying a piece of iron, such as a nail, with you when travelling near lochs and burns is a wise precaution to take!

## The Red Lion Rampant

The Red Lion Rampant is the second heraldic beast of Scotland and appears upon the Royal Standard flag. It is a symbol of royalty, strength, power and protection. As the unicorn represents the moon, so the red lion represents the sun, and magically speaking these two heraldic beasts together represent duality and the balance of nature.

Long associated with the monarchs of Scotland, the Red Lion Rampant stands tall upon his hind legs, daring anyone to come closer to the claws of his posturing forepaws! He represents courage, bravery and boldness and is a symbol of sovereignty. Robert the Bruce would have fought beneath this banner, as would Mary, Queen of Scots. Although technically these days it can only be flown by King Charles III at his royal palaces in Scotland, it is also widely sold as a souvenir too. So you can own the Royal Standard, as I do, you just can't fly it! That said, you can still invoke the spirit of the Red Lion Rampant for magical purposes.

### RED LION RAMPANT SPELL FOR COURAGE

Is there any creature more synonymous with courage than the lion? Probably not, which is why it a popular heraldic beast. The Red Lion Rampant can remind you of your own strength and bolster your courage in adversity. For this spell you will need some kind of image that represents the red lion of Scotland, be this a flag, a postcard or a print bought online. Alternatively, you can purchase lapel pins and jewellery from gifts shops in tourist spots across Scotland and on their websites. Once you have your image, take it to your altar, light a red candle and think of all that the red lion represents. Think of Robert the Bruce fighting for his crown, or William Wallace fighting for independence. Think of the courage and bravery shown by all the people who have fought and gone into battle beneath the image of this beast over the centuries. Close your eyes and tap into this strength, for it belongs to you too. Feel your heart swell with the pride of the red lion and then say these words:

⌘

*I call the red lion of tooth and claw*

*Downtrodden I will be no more*

*For my faults I shall atone*

*Let courage now fill my flesh and bone*

*I Rally to the Red Lion, Scotland's Pride*

*Now let us do or let us die!*

*As those before me have fought and fell*

*I share their courage; all doubt I repel*

*I stand my ground with strength and valour*

*And bring forth my courage from this hour.*

Allow the candle to burn down and feel free to repeat this spell whenever you are facing adversity or a particular challenge. Invoke the courage of the red lion and claim it for your own.

# The Welsh Dragon

Perhaps even older than the Red Lion Rampant is the Red Dragon of Wales, which is reputed to have been the royal standard of King Arthur himself. As their heraldic beast, the Red Dragon banner is flown all over Wales. In history it was of course the banner of Henry Tudor, father of Henry VIII, and was the banner he fought under to win his victory over Richard III at the Battle of Bosworth Field. This Tudor influence is still seen in the white and green background of the Welsh Flag – white and green were the colours of the House of Tudor. To this day, the Red Dragon is known as one of the King's Beasts. It is a symbol of power, wisdom, sovereignty and survival.

## HOW TO MAKE DRAGON'S BREATH INCENSE FOR WISDOM

For this spell you will need a mortar and pestle, a clean empty jar, a sticky label and pen, a selection of the following dried herbs: sage, mint, rosemary, basil. You will also need a loose incense burner and charcoal blocks.

Into the mortar place three tablespoons of each of the dried herbs. These herbs represent wisdom, clarity, protection and power. Grind them to a fine powder using the pestle. Once you have your blended incense, pour it into the jar and label it Dragon's Breath Incense.

Hold the jar in your hands and empower it by saying:

⌘

*Red Dragon of fiery might*

*Lend your wisdom, send your light*

*Celtic drake old and wise*

*May your breath filter truth from lies*

*Dragon's breath smoking free*

*Knowledge is power, so mote it be.*

Whenever you have need for greater wisdom, clarity or concentration, light a charcoal block in your incense burner and add three pinches of dragon's breath incense. Let the smoke curl round and wisdom abound.

## The Stoor Worm

Some Celtic legends have their root in Norse mythology, and they may have come across with the Vikings who invaded Britain and then decided to settle, bringing their stories with them. Some of the Celtic regions, such as the Shetlands and the Orkney Islands, were Norse to begin with and that is reflected in their folklore. These islands were gifted to Scotland by the king of Norway as part of a marriage dowry in the 1400's and they have been part of the British Isles ever since, although the islanders have kept many of their ancestral Nordic customs and cultural festivals.

The legend of the Stoor Worm, which is a creation myth, comes from Orkney and it has its roots in Nordic tales of a giant sea serpent called *Jörmungandr* or the Midgard Serpent. This mythical creature is a prime example of how the two cultures, both Norse and Celtic have merged together over time.

The Stoor Worm, sometimes called Mester Stoor Worm, is a giant sea dragon or serpent that is said to live in the waters around the far northern tip of Scotland. His breath is poisonous and can kill a man who gets too close, while his mighty barbed tail can swipe out an entire village in seconds. Furthermore, the Stoor Worm demands a diet of sacrificial maidens – at least seven young women each month were to be fed to the serpent to appease him and keep him from destroying the local coastal villages. Many brave warriors tried to defeat the Stoor Worm but to no avail. He was too powerful and strong for any sword.

Eventually along came a young farm boy named Assipattle who was clever enough to carry with him a piece of smouldering peat burning in a bucket when he faced the monster. As the Stoor Worm swallowed Assipattle whole, he thrust the burning peat

into the sea dragon's innards! When the Stoor Worm vomited from the pain, Assipattle was thrown back into the sea, alive and well, where he swam to shore and married the king's daughter. The Stoor Worm died of his injuries from the burning peat and so he troubled the people no more. As the giant sea monster died, his teeth and head became the Shetland and Orkney Isles, while his great body became Iceland, where his stomach still smoulders and rumbles to this day, in the form of a great volcano.

## Arderyn Y Corff – Corpse Bird

Welsh folklore tells of the corpse bird, Arderyn Y Corff, which is a supernatural creature of avian appearance. Unlike real birds however, this bird has no feathers and appears to be completely bald. It is known as the corpse bird because it is said to be an omen of death. When someone is about to die, the Arderyn Y Corff is said to sit outside their door and chirp in mourning for their passing. Being a spirit bird, it can pass through locked doors, coming straight into the house where it will take up its vigil outside the door of the doomed person's room. Its mournful chirping has an otherworldly echo, which resonates throughout the house, alerting the household to its message. It is said that the bird's chirp sounds much like the Welsh word for 'come' as it calls out to its target, "*Come, come!*". In this sense, it is a psychopomp waiting to guide the soon-to-be deceased person's soul into the next world, beyond the veil of death. The Arderyn Y Corff could be the root of the superstition that a bird tapping on a window portends a death in the house, or that a bird flying into the house brings bad luck.

## Cait-Sith

The cait-sith is a fairy cat of Celtic folklore. As a spectral cat, it can be either good or bad luck depending on where you see it. In Ireland, it was said to be a black cat with a white spot on its chest and was considered bad luck. However, in the Highlands of Scotland it is more ambiguous. Here it is said to be a pure white spirit cat, with a spectral glow around it. While some believe it to be a bad omen, others claim it brings good fortune if it crosses your path. Another belief is that to see one by day is good luck, but by dark it bodes ill. Some say that the cait-sith will steal your soul as you sleep, while for others, she is a warning of someone holding harmful intent towards you. Whatever the truth, this simple spell will keep the cait-sith happy and your fortune good.

## Cait-Sith Samhain Spell

On the night of Samhain, take a saucer of fresh milk and place it on the doorstep. Next to this, place a few springs of dried catnip. Now repeat this blessing three times:

⌘

*Cait-sith of fairy light*

*Bring no harm or ill this night*

*Accept these gifts of comfort and glee*

*Blessings be upon me and thee*

## Grimalkin

Another spirit cat and cousin to the cait-sith, is the grimalkin. This Celtic legend could have been inspired by sightings of the Scottish wild cat. A grimalkin is a grey or grey-striped cat. It is said to be a trickster, but will befriend young children, though it doesn't like men! During the witch hunts of Scotland, grey cats, or grimalkins, were often thought to be witches in disguise and so cats of this colour became very distrusted and mistreated as a result. Legend states that grimalkins prefer the company of women and would frequently move in with solitary widows, adding fuel to the fire of the witch craze. Although not considered unlucky as such, if you were a woman living with a grey cat in the Highlands at the time, your odds of survival weren't that great! The grimalkin was so aligned with witches, that 'grimalkin' became a derogatory term for an old lady or an out-spoken woman. You can call on the grimalkin if you are being maligned in any way. Light a grey candle or a simple tea-light and say:

⌘

*Grimalkin, grimalkin uncross my path*

*Let those who malign me feel your wrath!*

*Ashes to ashes and dust to dust*

*The past dead and buried, free from mistrust*

*As I walk my own path, I will have my own say*

*Grimalkin protect me through each fight and fray.*

## Cù-Sìth

It isn't only cats that the Celts were superstitious about, but dogs too. The cù-sìth is a fairy dog that tramps the Highlands and Islands of Scotland and Ireland. Some believe that he is a hound of the Wild Hunt, looking for prey, while others say he is simply out looking for unwary night-time travellers so he can steal their souls. He is a large hound, with a shaggy coat that has an unearthly greenish hue and green light coming from it, denoting his role as a fairy dog. His English counterparts would be the Barguest Hound, Black Shuck, the Grim and Old Padfoot. Like them he is considered to be an omen of death or misfortune, so should you hear the sound of panting and heavy paws coming up behind you, it is said that you should take refuge in the nearest kirk, without looking back. Despite his bad reputation, he is nonetheless a messenger. He barks three times in warning: one bark indicates that the bad luck can be avoided, two barks that the misfortune is destined but a necessary lesson, while three barks is an omen of death. Like most hell-hound legends, the curse of the cù-sìth can be thwarted by crossing a body of water, be it a loch, burn or stream, so all is not lost. Simply hop over a puddle and you're home and dry!

## Auld Nessie

Quite possibly the most famous Celtic beast of all is of course Auld Nessie, or the Loch Ness Monster. Nessie is an ancient water beast said to be living in the depths of Loch Ness in the Scottish Highlands. She was first sighted as far back as the 6th century by St Columba. There have been many more sightings reported over the years, but some have proved to be no more than a hoax. That said, people still travel from across the globe for the chance of seeing Nessie breaching the surface of the loch, but she is a shy creature and tends to keep to the depths. However, legend states that offering her a wee dram in libation can improve your chances of making her acquaintance. Simply pour a small amount of whisky into the waters of Loch Ness and wait to see if you can spot the famous long neck and triple humps of Auld Nessie. Slainte!

# Celtic Meditation: Unburden Your Heart at Urquart

*You find yourself standing on the banks of Loch Ness on a late summer's evening. The full moon is rising, casting a glow upon the water. The heat of a golden summer's day still hangs in the air and midges dart and dash at the water's edge. Beside you there is a little row of stone cottages, and the ruin of Urquart Castle stands as sentry, watching over the loch as it has always done, ever since the days when it was a vibrant seat of power and a stronghold of the Highlands. Its derelict walls glow silvery in the moonlight and its solemn stones seem to offer you comfort, as you sit down by the side of the loch and sigh.*

*Your heart feels heavy with sorrow and the surrounding beauty only serves to remind you of all that you have lost, all that you once believed in and of that which is no more. Betrayal, heartbreak, grief and neglect all weigh on you, keeping your spirits low, your tongue sharp, your fuse short and your mind distrustful. You wonder if you will ever get over the sadness that has overwhelmed you in recent times. You wonder how you could ever have believed that your life would turn out any different from this, how you could ever have been so foolish as to trust the one who made false promises, who once held your heart, only to cast it aside and grind it to dust and ashes beneath their well-heeled, highly polished boot.*

*A sound makes you look around to see a man coming out of one of the cottages nearby. You flinch from the prospect of human contact, shrinking back into the shadow of the castle walls, but he makes no move, not a single step, towards you. He doesn't see you at all. He simply stands on the doorstep for a moment, smoking a cigarette as he looks out over the loch, surveying the historic landscape with all the indifference of one who belongs here, blind to the beauty that surrounds him because he sees it every day. Then he turns and goes back inside, indifferent to the world outside of his own existence and oblivious to your pain.*

*Alone once more, you sigh in relief – the deep relief that only solitude brings. You feel too sad to chat with a stranger, too raw to connect with anyone just now, too hurt to be healed, too wounded to be forgiving. You weep for the hopelessness of it all. Let the battle be fought another day – for now, there is only sorrow and bitter disappointment. For now, there is only emptiness where the fight should be, and darkness where love once shone so brightly. The valour will come, in time. You will live to fight another day, and you will know victory once more. You will overcome the sting of betrayal and heartbreak, but not today, not tonight.*

*Tonight you will sit with your grief and allow the tears to fall into the waters of Loch Ness as you process the pain of what you've experienced, as you come to terms with the prospect of empty days stretching out before you, now that your love has gone, flying their true colours all the way. Absent-mindedly, you pick up a small stone and toss it across the water, watching the ripples as it skips over the surface before sinking into the depths below.*

*"So sinks my love," you say to yourself. You pick up another pebble and skim this across the water too. "So sinks my trust," you say as the second pebble sinks. Next you find the biggest pebble you can*

*hold in your hand and standing up, you throw it into the loch with all of your might, crying out "So sinks our future together! Good riddance and be gone! I'm done with you!" You watch the large pebble splash into the water and the ripples expanding in circles. But then, instead of diminishing, the ripples get wider and wider, the circles creating a vortex. You watch open mouthed, bewildered by what is happening in the water, until all at once a head appears, followed by a slender neck and the humps of a sea creature – the Loch Ness Monster is here!*

*Her skin shimmers in the moonlight, iridescent in shades of pale blue and green, sliver and lilac. You gape in astonishment as she swims towards you, her neck stretched out to greet you. "You called, Seeker?"*

*"I…I did?"*

*"Of course you did – why else would you skim three pebbles in the waters of Loch Ness, if not to summon me for assistance? Though I have to say that last pebble – known as **a rock** to the rest of us! – that was a wee bit harsh. Remind me not to get on **your** wrong side! Who's been upsetting **you**, eh?"*

*"I didn't know I was calling anyone. I was just frustrated. I'm sorry I disturbed you."*

*"Frustrated and **sad**. Heartbroken, even. Come now, tell Nessie all about it. Unburden your heart to me, Seeker, let's see what we can do to make you feel better." Nessie settles down in the shallows of the water and lowers her head to listen. You find yourself telling her all about your sorrow and heartbreak, all about the betrayals*

*you have suffered and the one who has let you down repeatedly, letting her know exactly how you feel. It feels good to let go of all the emotions you've been holding in for some time. You weep as you talk, hopeless and despondent. "I feel like my life is over now that my love is gone!" you say, "I feel like I'll never have the future I once dreamt of. It's all ruined. Gone forever!"*

*"Oh come now, this isn't like you Seeker. You cannot let those who betrayed you damage your prospects for a good life. Of course someone else will come along – and even if they don't, well there's no shame in being single you know. Look at me – I haven't look at another sea-creature in centuries and I'm happy enough. You don't* ***have*** *to go through the world two by two you know. Trust me, the right one will turn up when you least expect it. And the one who betrayed you? Well, they weren't the right one after all were they? If they were, they would have cherished you, and the pure, loving, loyal heart you gave to them. They would have worshipped the water you swam on! Your heart was too big for them, that's all."*

*"But I feel like I'll never get over them, like they will always have a hold on me, a piece of me and I'll never be able to move on," you admit.*

*"Nonsense. You just need to learn to swim with someone else. You need to let go of the emotions that tie you to them and I have just the thing for it." Nessie dips her head into the water and pulls out a large shell. "Here, Seeker, take this. Now I want you to breathe all your troubles and sorrows into the shell. Speak them out loud into the shell if you like, or blow them into it, but just get it all out of your system. Ready?" You nod and lift the shell to your lips. "On you go then." Nessie encourages. You do as she bids you, blowing all your sorrows into the shell, in sigh after sigh. Your tears fall and as they touch the shell, it sparkles like quicksilver. Suddenly you begin to feel so much lighter. Now that the sorrow has been released, it feels like all the fighting spirit is coming back into your soul. You will not let heartbreak ruin your life! You will not carry*

*the one who betrayed you, any further! You will live your life with joy and optimism and love, going forward. You will rise above this, just as you have risen above everything else you have faced in your life. "Excellent!" says Nessie. "Now hand the shell to me."*

*"What will you do with it?" you ask.*

*"I'll take it back to the bottom of the loch and carry your troubles away with it where they can be cleansed with a good dose of salt water."*

*"Thank you. I appreciate your help. I have a small favour to ask, if that's alright?"*

*"Name it."*

*"The one I loved and lost – take care of them for me. Watch over them."*

*"Ah, Seeker, your heart's far too big for them, but aye, I'll keep an eye on them for you. I'll make sure they know what they've missed out on too! Every time they see me, they'll be reminded of what they did to* **you***." You nod in response, grateful to have Nessie's cooperation. "And now Seeker, you must leave your sorrows behind and go back to your own realm. Climb the hill up to the ruins of Urquart Castle and it will take you home. Farewell, Seeker, you know where to find me if you need me again." You thank Nessie, who is certainly no monster, and you begin to climb the banks of Urquart, going up, up, up and away from the heartache, up through the ruins of former splendour, up and away from your past pain and back into the glimmer of your waking life.*

## Chapter Eight

# Celtic Romance

**For all their warlike characteristics, the Celts also have a reputation for being quite romantic. In a landscape of majestic mountains and misty glens, of full moons rising over beautiful lochs or casting shadows on Pictish stones and ancient castles, it's hard not to become a romantic! The Celtic landscape simply oozes romance and stories of star-crossed lovers such as Scáthach and Cucullain, are prolific in Celtic folklore.**

This deep sense of romance infiltrates modern relationships too, with phases such as '*taking the moonlight*' and '*Anam Cara*' being commonplace in Celtic regions. In this chapter we will explore some aspects of Celtic romance and look at ways in which you can invoke more of it into your own life. We begin with the Celtic view of soul mates...

## Anam Cara

Anam Cara is a Gaelic phrase which simply means '*soul friend*' but there is far more to such a relationship than mere friendship. An Anam Cara relationship is complex, intense and frequently romantic in nature. Sexual tension is strong and ever present between the two parties. This is the Celtic version of twin flames, but with the added pressure that an Anam Cara relationship rarely runs smoothly. There are often many obstacles in the way before the two lovers are free to be together, but once there, their commitment to one another is unshakable and everlasting.

This is because an Anam Cara relationship is thought to be a commitment the couple made in the spirit realms; a promise that their souls would find one another in this life no matter what. This commitment means that all earthly obstacles become less significant, because it is *a love above all loves*.

While such obstacles might be inconvenient and frustrating, in the end the couple trust in the value of their love and in the fated success of an Anam Cara, spiritual bond. In short they believe that they are destined to be together and nothing and no-one can prevent it.

Having said that, this type of relationship does have its drawbacks. Firstly, it cuts people off from other possibilities for romantic happiness as they are too invested in their Anam Cara – their *one true love*. Secondly it means that the couple have greater potential to hurt one another, because their investment is absolute, so the potential for heartbreak along the road to happiness is significant and something to consider. It is still a lovely concept though and something many people still aspire to.

If you want to draw your Anam Cara to you, cast the spell below, but be aware that such a love affair is not without its difficulties and the road ahead may be rocky before it leads you both to your happy ever after. Good luck!

# Spell to Summon Your Anam Cara

You will need two small paper hearts about 2cm squared, one pink and one red, a red pen, a red candle, red thread and a sewing needle. As darkness falls light the candle and say:

⌘

*By burning flame my love is true*

*Wherever you are I call out to you*

*My Anam Cara, my Anam Cara, my Anam Cara*

Hold an image in your mind of your Anam Cara, your soul mate, and write your own name on the pink heart and the words Anam Cara on the red heart. Thread the needle and knot the end of the thread. Next pierce the pink heart from underneath, with your name facing upwards, using the needle and draw the thread through, right up to the knot. Say:

⌘

*I pierce my own heart in love and light*

*To summon my Anam Cara to me on this night*

Next pierce the red heart from underneath, with Anam Cara facing downwards and sandwiched with your name, and say:

⌘

*I pierce my Anam Cara's heart in love and light*

*I summon him/her to me from this night*

Finally, remove the needle, wrap the reminder of the thread around the two hearts and seal the end with a little melted wax from the candle. This is your love talisman and it will help to draw your Anam Cara towards you and into your life. To complete the spell, hold tight to the hearts and repeat this chant nine times:

⌘

*By burning flame these hearts are true,*

*Wherever you are I now summon you*

*My Anam Cara, my Anam Cara, my Anam Cara!*

Keep the hearts with you at all times to draw your soul friend into your life. Allow the candle to burn down naturally.

## The Fairy Lover

Of course, not everyone is looking for a love as intense as the Anam Cara variety. Some people are looking for something a bit more casual. A brief fling with a Fairy Lover might be just the ticket! In Celtic folklore the Fairy Lover is a fey companion who offers affection, adoration and sexual gratification for a limited time only. They seemingly appear out of nowhere and make an immediate bee-line for their romantic target. The sabbats are a prime time to meet such a lover or to call one into your life for a brief encounter. They tend to disappear just as fast as they arrived and you will never hear from them again, for they have returned to the world of Elphame or the fairy realms. Their sudden appearance/disappearance is one of the signs that you have attracted the attentions of a Fairy Lover. They might also be extraordinarily good looking and have green eyes or slightly pointed ears – clues as to their fey background.

A Fairy Lover isn't a lifelong companion. They are a brief encounter, an ego boost, a healing balm for a broken heart or an interlude to loneliness. They give you the confidence you need to get back in the game of love and romance. Like two ships that pass in the night, they will come when you have romantic need of them, never to be seen again. However, their magic will stay with you in the form of the sweet memories you made together and the confidence they imbued in you. Cast the following spell to summon a Fairy Lover into your life for a casual affair or a healing interlude.

## Spell to Summon a Fairy Lover

This spell is most effective when cast into the sea by the light of the full moon, but any natural body of water will suffice. You will need a pebble. Hold this in your hand as you walk by the water, enjoying the sound of the lapping water or rolling waves. As you hold the pebble to your heart, close your eyes and imagine a fairy lover walking towards you and sweeping you off your feet. Now say the following incantation three times:

⌘

*Galatea, Melusine, Aphrodite; Merrow Maids, all*

*Send out a Fairy Lover, to hold me in thrall*

*To thrill and delight me, to tantalize me*

*To heal and calm me, to offer sweet balm to me*

*To sweep me away before break of day*

*To love me and leave me but never deceive me*

*What once was yours I return to thee*

*As a Fairy Lover comes forth to me!*

Throw the pebble into the water, preferably on the seventh wave of an incoming tide, and walk away from the water without looking back. Look out for your fairy lover who should appear suddenly within seven days.

## The Seelie and Unseelie Courts

The Seelie Court is a term given to the fairies in Scottish folklore. Also known as Trooping Fairies, these fey beings are the highest of the elementals, with both a king and queen, plus noble knights among them. They are famous for holding elaborate balls and revels in fairy hills, stone circles and barrow mounds and they are said to troop about the countryside at the time of the full moon and on sabbats. They ride magical steeds such as unicorns and kelpies and they march in Troops, from one fairy residence to another. They tend to look kindly on humans and will help them if requested to. However, their cousins are less friendly, for the counterpart to the Seelie Court is the Unseelie Court, which is comprised of dark fairies and troublemakers. Any Fairy that has been cast out of the Seelie Court is likely to be welcomed at the Unseelie Court, where they play tricks on humans and cause as much trouble as they can for their more benevolent cousins. It is possible that the Scottish Seelie and Unseelie Courts are a version of the Irish fey court, the Tuatha Dé Dannan.

## The Fair Knight

The Fair Knight, also known as the Fairy Knight, is an otherworldly knight who rides around the country looking for adventure and performing acts of valour, or sometimes trickery. In most legends, he is someone who has magical or regenerative ability, such as the Green Knight in the tale of *Sir Gawain and the Green Knight*. In other versions of this legend the Fair Knight is one who used to be human, but who was snatched away to the fairy realms where he earns his spurs through personal and magical transformation. We see this in the Scottish legend, *The Tale of Tam Lin*. Some Fair Knights are aligned with particular seasons, and they can be members of either the Seelie or the Unseelie Court, or simply a solitary figure with no allegiance to any, depending on the legend. Whoever the Fair Knight is, he often falls in love with a mortal woman who has to accomplish seemingly impossible tasks to prove herself worthy of becoming his bride.

## Taking the Moonlight

*Taking the moonlight* is the act of courting outdoors. Being asked the question '*Will you take the moonlight with me tonight?*' simply means will you meet up after dark for a snog! While not everyone will be lucky enough to experience being courted among the misty glens, lochs and mountains of a Celtic landscape, you can nonetheless tap into this romantic tradition by casting this general love spell, inspired by the Celtic tradition of taking the moonlight.

Light a tea-light and spend some time imagining your dream date. What would you wear, where would you go, how would you feel?

Picture it all, then when you are ready say the incantation below three times:

⌘

*I summon a lover to explore the night*

*Together in love, taking the moonlight*

*I summon a lover to brighten my days*

*Together in joy, by sunshine haze*

*I summon a lover day by day*

*He/she moves ever closer, coming my way.*

*I summon a lover to share the old ways*

*Taking the moonlight amid silver rays*

*So shall it be*

Let the tea-light burn down and keep an eye open for romantic opportunities coming your way.

# Auld Lang Syne Spell for a Lost Love

To get a second chance with a lost love write a note as to why you want to try with them again and what you have learnt from your mistakes. Burn this note and repeat the chant three times:

⌘

*For Auld Lang Syne, for old time's sake*

*I spell of reunion I would make*

*Casting out through smoke and air*

*(Name) come back to me, good times to share*

*You will hear my call from miles away*

*Come back to me and return to stay*

*Spirit to spirit and heart to heart*

*No longer shall we be apart*

*I am dear to you, you are dear to me*

*Together again, so mote it be.*

## St. Andrew's Love Spell

St. Andrew is of course the patron saint of Scotland and his saint's day is celebrated on the 30th of November each year. This traditional love spell calls on St. Andrew to bring about a love connection. It can be performed at any time on St. Andrew's Day. Light a tea-light candle and write the following traditional incantation out on a slip of paper, then chant the words out loud three times in all:

⌘

*I have a wish, a wish for a kiss*

*From a lover in a kilt, looking all fine*

*I cast this wish, this wish for a kiss*

*And by St, Andrew, this lover is mine!*

Allow the tea-light to burn down naturally and carry the spell paper with you wherever you go. Remember that love is always a surprise, so expect the unexpected and be open to new encounters – especially if they happen to be wearing a kilt!

# Celtic Meditation: A Pagan Rite Upon a Pictish Stone

*You find yourself standing at the foot of a hill on a clear winter night. The stars are shining brightly above you and there is the lingering smell of petrichor in the air. You set off walking up the steep track of the hill. This time, you know exactly where you are going, and you walk with purpose and excitement. The track is slick with mud, and you slip and slide your way up the hillside. You know that someone is waiting for you at the top and you are eager to meet them.*

*Pausing for a moment, you glance up at the summit and see the dark shadow of a solitary stone jutting out of the hilltop. That is your goal, your destination and you set off once more, with even more determination. It's a long and tiring walk, but eventually you summit the hill and there before you is the stone.*

*It is ancient and covered in moss and lichen. The moonlight makes the stone gleam, the damp rock sparkling from an earlier rainfall. You hear a gentle humming sound coming from the stone and smile to yourself. You have heard the stone singing before and you know what it means. It is welcoming you to the magical hill and the history upon which it stands so proudly, even centuries after it was first erected. There are deep marks within the stone, and you trace the decorative carvings with your fingers. A bird's head, an eagle, once carved by a master craftsman of the Picts, is still visible today. This Pictish stone is a sacred link between now and then, and you feel the pull of the past, which draws you back here, again and again. The stone offers you comfort and strength, a solid reminder of reassurance that all that once was, still remains.*

*All at once you sense that you are not alone. Sure enough, you feel arms wrapping around you from behind in a safe, protective embrace. "It's good to see you Seeker," whispers a voice in your ear, a voice you would know among a thousand others. "I've been waiting for you."*

*"I know. I came as soon as I could." You try to turn around, but the arms hold you fast. "Don't try to see me, Seeker. Just stay with me for a moment or two."*

*"Why can't I see you?" you ask.*

*"Because I am your Anam Cara. You know that. You must wait to see me until we meet in life. I'm looking for you too, you know."*

*"I know," you sigh and lean back against your soul mate. "What must I do to find you?"*

*"Make your heart ready for me. Let go of past loves and past pains. Let go of expectations of what I am or who I am. Just allow your heart to recognise me. You heart understands mine, Seeker, as mine understands yours. That is the only truth you need to recognise me."*

*"I will try, but it's so hard, waiting," you sigh.*

*"It's hard for me too. But open the door to your heart and I will come to you. We have a soul contract, you and I, to love one another across lifetimes. Such a journey was never going to be easy. It is worth taking time over, Seeker. It is worth waiting for."*

*"I know." The two of you stand in silence for a time, then your Anam Cara says, "Give me your hand, my love." Your soul mate turns your hand palm up and with a sharp blade, makes a small cut, which they repeat on their own palm. You clasp hands, allowing the blood of your two Clans to mingle as your Anam Cara says, "Blood of my blood, I summon thee. Blood of my blood, I will return to thee." You repeat the words, then you both seal the vow by wiping your mingled blood upon the sacred Pictish marriage stone, which absorbs the offering instantly.*

*"Now, Seeker, look up." You do as you are bidden and gasp to see the swirling illumination of the northern lights, shining high above you in the sky. "See, the Mirrie Dances are out for us tonight! Now, whenever you see them, you will think of me and know that I will find you, in this life and the next. Have faith, Seeker, as you go back to your own realm." You feel a kiss on your cheek, then once more you are alone, gazing at the stone that now holds your promise to your soul mate. After a few moments of reflection, you turn and walk back down the hill, away from the stone and down, down, down, back into your waking life, where your Anam Cara has promised to find you.*

Chapter Nine

# By Root and Branch, Leaf and Tree

The Celts had a strong affinity with trees and the Druid priests would commune with them and use them in magic and divination. To the Celts trees were more than just plants and vegetation – they were deities in their own right, each tree signifying particular traits and omens. Trees provided fuel for the fire, wood for making weapons such as spears and bows, or currachs which were the canoe-like boats used by the Celtic tribes. They offered shelter from harsh weather for livestock and sturdy thatch for croft-houses.

Vast parts of the Celtic regions were covered in great forests, from what is now the Black Forest in Germany to the great Caledonian and Snowdonian forests in the UK. Wildlife such as deer and boar, could be hunted in the forest for meat and the spirit of Cernunnos would have been honoured in the woods. The Druids would have foraged amid the trees for medicinal plants to heal their tribes, while the women and children would have picked berries and so on to formulate early dyes for cloth and wool. Trees were an intrinsic aspect of Celtic life and a vital resource for survival, so it is hardly surprising that the Celts invented their own 13-month calendar using trees which we will explore shortly.

## Nemeton Glade – A Sacred Grove

A *nemeton* is a scared place that offers a natural sense of sanctuary. Glades were open spaces within a glen or strath, while groves were clearings amid the forest, a space within the woods that was clear enough you could light a fire without danger. Groves, glades and glens were nemetons, places to gather round for entertainment, war councils and debates. Here in the Grove, the Celts would have held celebrations and sabbat festivities. It was a place of power, where elders would pass on their wisdom, betrothals would be announced and youngsters would play, with the trees bearing witness.

We still feel echoes of the nemeton when we walk through a woodland and suddenly start to feel relaxed, uplifted, exhilarated and happy. Our troubles fall away and we enjoy being out in nature, in a sacred space surrounded by trees. That is the nemeton effect and it is one that our Celtic ancestors would have been very familiar with. You can recreate this effect by planting trees around the edge of your garden if you have one, thus creating your own Grove and nemeton space for magic and meditation. Or use potted plants as an alternative. Consider planting trees that were sacred to the Celts, using their Tree Calendar as inspiration.

## The Celtic Tree Calendar

For the Celts, the months of the year were ruled by trees. Here you can see that each tree was also attributed magical significance and energies.

### BIRCH/BETH – 24 Dec–20 Jan

The birch was considered to be a cleansing tree. Its bark would be burnt in a ritual fire to ward off bad luck, ill health or any blight on the livestock. It was also considered to be a transitional tree, marking the passing of the darkest time of year. In divination, the birch tree meant that you should reflect inwards and make a fresh start.

### ROWAN/LUIS – 21 Jan–17 Feb

Rowan is of course famous for being the *uncrossing* tree – that is, it is said to guard against witches and negative energies, although many witches actually use rowan in their spells to ward off bad vibes. An equal armed cross of rowan twigs, tied with red thread and hung outside the door to the house was said to prevent negative energies taking root in the home and would protect the household from ill and bane.

### ASH/FEARN – 18 Feb–17 March

The Ash tree was thought to represent the three realms of past, present and future. It was therefore a fortune-telling tree and one which the Druids would meditate beneath to facilitate visions. A popular wood for Druid wands, the Ash Grove was said to be the most powerful nemeton of all.

## ALDER/SAILLE – 18 March–14 April

The Alder is the symbol of duality because it has both male and female catkins. It represents balance and polarity, light and dark, summer and winter. It reminds us that we cannot have one without the other, that life is governed by balance in all things. In divination, the alder tree would indicate that you need to redress the balance in your own life.

## WILLOW/ NION – 15 April–12 May

Willow is the tree of emotion, dreams and visons. It is flexible and so denotes that sometimes one must bend, so as not to be broken. It is about give and take, ebb and flow, the waxing and waning of the moon. A very feminine tree, the willow represents female strength and resilience. It is a message to trust your intuition and to show compassion and empathy for others. It is the tree of kindness.

## HAWTHORNE/HUATH – 13 May–9 June

This is a tree of protection and wherever one grows the area is protected by the goddess. Its thorns are sharp, its berries poisonous and its blossom is the herald of spring. It is a very magical tree and to cut one down is considered to be bad luck. However, to care for one and offer it regular libations of cider or ale is said to have the opposite effect and will bring many blessings. It is however bad luck to bring hawthorn blossom into the house.

## OAK/DUIR – 10 June–7 July

The tree of Cernunnos! The oak is symbolic of strength, wisdom and the Celtic god. To the ancient Druids, the regal oak was simply the King of the Woods and a tree which represented the sovereignty of the land. Oak trees were also considered to be portals, or doorways, to other realms. It is the tree most strongly associated with the months of summer.

### HOLLY/TINNE – 8 July–4 August

The holly now marks the passing of summer and the return of the darker half of the year. Although strongly associated with winter, magically the holly begins to come into its own in late summer. Again it is a protective tree and is said to bring good luck, especially if it bears many berries. Bringing holly into the home during the time of the winter solstice is said to protect the household throughout the depths of winter and the coldest months of the year. Offer the tree a libation in late summer and wassail it in winter to bring its blessings to you. As an evergreen tree of winter it is linked to the Cailleach.

### HAZEL/COLL – 5 Aug–1 Sep

The hazel tree was sacred to the Druids who would eat the nuts to bring about prophetic visions. Hazel nuts were also fed to those who were about to be sacrificed. These trees are symbols of wisdom and the unknown. They represent prophecy, psychic visons and prophetic dreaming.

### BRAMBLE/MUIN–2 Sep – 29 Sep

Bramble is the plant of resilience, stubbornness and obstinacy – and if you've ever tried to rid your garden of them, you will know why! Brambles are prickly and vicious, yet they also offer an abundance of autumn fruit, so they symbolise both sacrifice and prosperity. Bramble also symbolises fertility and virility. It is a plant that is strongest in the autumn months and is therefore associated with the autumnal equinox.

### IVY/GORT – 30 Sep – 27 Oct

Ever twining, ever binding, ivy symbolises dependence and smothering. As a feminine plant, it reminds us that there is a fine line between nurturing and suffocating! It is a warning not to become a clinging vine, but to maintain your independence. As an evergreen plant, it represents the Cailleach and her grip on the world in winter.

### REED/NGETAL – 28 Oct–24 Nov

Reeds were used as early writing implements so this plant symbolises language, poetics, the written word and the scribe. They were also fashioned into pipes, so they symbolise musicality too. They represent knowledge, learning, academics, the Arts, studying and wisdom. Reed reminds us that we are always learning, every day and that the quest for knowledge is never really over.

### ELDER/RUIS – 25 Nov–23 Dec

Elder, the magical thirteenth tree, is the tree of the Crone. It symbolises magic, spellcasting, healing, the fairy realms and the unknown. The Elder was a wise mother figure to the Celts and a symbol of the goddess. It was considered very bad luck to cut one down, though harvesting berries and blossoms was acceptable, providing one had asked the Elder Mother's permission first.

## The Sacred Triad

Whilst in England the sacred triad is made up of oak, ash and thorn, in Scottish Pecti Wita, the sacred triad is made up of thistle, heather and pine. Using these plants in your rituals is a good way to bring a touch of Wita to your spells and each plant has its own special meaning.

The thistle is the emblem of Scotland. Its motto is '*None shall irritate me unscathed*' and it is prickly enough to make its presence felt and administer immediate retribution if tampered with. In Wita, thistles were said to be masculine plants and were associated with the Horned God, Cernunnos. They are a visual reminder of strength, resilience and courage. Wearing thistle jewellery can help you to tap into these virtues.

Heather is a pretty flowering plant that grows in abundance across Scotland, turning the Highlands purple when in full flower. It is the feminine counterpart to the Scottish thistle, being linked with the ancient queen, Scotia, for whom Scotland is named. Wearing a sprig of heather is said to bring good fortune and to ensure you are blessed by the Fae.

Scots pine is a fragrance we are all familiar with, as it is used to scent many products, from candles to bath salts. Pine grows abundantly in the rich Caledonian forests. There is great majesty to these trees and the forests where they grow have a very special nemeton atmosphere. Burning pine incense or essential oil would help to bring the spirit of Caledonia to your rituals.

## The Clootie Tree

High on a hill in Inverness, overlooking the Cromarty Firth and Fort George, stands a colourful clootie tree. This is a tree that has been made into a *wishing tree* by the local people. Tradition states that should you ever come across a clootie tree you are entitled to request a single boon from the tree spirit. In return you must leave an item of clothing that you are wearing. To activate the boon, simply tie the item of clothing or clootie, meaning cloth, to a branch of the tree as you make your wish. Then walk away and do not look back. The spirit of the tree will grant your wish if it comes from the heart and causes no harm. The Clootie tree in Inverness is covered in scarves, gloves and socks, but you don't need to travel that far to tap into this old Celtic tradition. Simply find a friendly looking tree and turn it into a clootie tree by hanging the first item of clothing on its

branches and making your wish. You could use a tree in your garden or a local woodland. This is an old tradition, similar to that of well dressing. The sabbats are always a good time to visit or create a clootie tree, alternatively visit the tree on the night of the full moon. Clootie trees are not exclusive to Scotland, so do some research and see if there is such a tree in your local area. If not, start a family tradition with a tree in your garden, or even a sturdy house plant on which you tie ribbons instead of clothing. In this way you are honouring the Celtic tradition of the magical wishing tree. Take special care of the tree and spend time tending it.

## Celtic Meditation:
## **Queen of Druids**

*You find yourself back in the Caledonian forest, wandering through trees and enjoying the nature all around you. Pushing through the branches you come once more to the grove, the clearing where you last met Cernunnos. He is not here today and nor are his beloved deer. Instead, there is a woman, sitting in the middle of the grove. She wears a white robe and a silver moon crown shines upon her brow as she rests, cross-legged on the grass, her eyes closed in serene meditation. She is a druid and from the crown on her head, you know her to be Druantia, Queen of the Druids.*

*You take another step and a twig snaps. Her eyes flick open, and she smiles at you. "Merry meet, lady...", you begin, but Druantia puts a finger to her lips, telling you to be quiet. She motions to you to sit beside her, and you do so. "It is a lovely grove...", you begin again, but once more Druantia puts her finger to her lips and admonishes you to remain silent, then she closes her eyes and continues her meditation. You follow her lead, closing your eyes and resting your hands gently on your knees. As you sit in silent meditation you feel the natural world come to the fore. Your mind wanders occasionally, but the sounds of nature are restful, bringing peace to your heart. You concentrate on your breathing and rest your thoughts, focusing only on the natural sounds around you – the breeze in the trees, the birdsong, the odd scuffle of the red squirrels as they leap from branch to branch and tree to tree.*

*As your body relaxes, it feels rooted in the earth. There are no words, no conversation between you and the druid queen, just silence, gentle companionship and the sounds of nature. You focus on one of the sounds around you and hone in on it. Now you understand. Druantia is teaching you the art of stillness and the gift of silence. You remain here for as long as you choose, in calm, silent meditation.*

*Eventually Druantia stands up and waits for you to complete your own meditation. You stand and smile at her, nodding. You needed the stillness much more than you realised. The druid queen presses a small wooden disk into your hand and looking down you notice that it is carved with a symbol from the Celtic tree calendar. You understand the meaning of the symbol and her message, and you nod your thanks. Then Druantia turns and begins to walk out of the grove, with you following behind, but as she walks, she begins to fade away, a walking phantom who leaves you right back where you began, back and back, back in your waking life once more, rested and refreshed.*

## Chapter Ten
# Wind and Stone

**The Celts have left us a legacy of beautiful artwork and standing stones. These stones are generally carved with intricate designs known as Celtic Knot-work, and totem animals such as eagles, stags, wolves and so on. Although the elements have weathered away some of these designs over the centuries, others can still be seen quite clearly.**

The Eagle Stone in Strathpeffer in the Scottish Highlands, is a Pictish stone that bears the carving of an eagle's head. Legend states that if this stone falls over three times, disaster will befall the town. This is typical of standing stones – there is always an accompanying legend or story to tell surrounding them. Other notable stones include the Ring of Brodgar; the Standing Stones of Callanish; the Nine Maidens Circle; Arbor Low Circle and Barrow Mound; and of course, Stonehenge. People travel from all over the world to see these sacred sites. In this chapter we will look at the magic of stones and how they can be used in spell-craft to tap into the magic of the Celts.

# The Celtic Cross

One form of stone craft that is synonymous with the Celts is the cross. A Celtic cross can be identified by the circle that is incorporated at the head of the cross and the intricate carvings that decorate it. It symbolises our connection with the earth and sky, the four winds and the four directions. For this reason, it is known as a cross which represents '*the parting and the meeting of the ways*'. Celtic crosses were often found at crossroads and were popular meeting places. It is a symbol older than Christianity, although it was adopted by early Christians and was displayed in kirks and churches. It is still a much beloved symbol, though it represents different things to different people. In Celtic magic it is a symbol of the four directions, their elements and associations, as follows:

**North:** the direction of Earth, symbolising abundance, prosperity and growth.

**East:** the direction of Air, symbolising intellect, new beginnings, creativity and communication.

**South:** the direction of Fire, symbolising passion, love, adventure and dynamic relationships.

**West:** the direction of Water, symbolising intuition, psychic powers, emotions, fluidity.

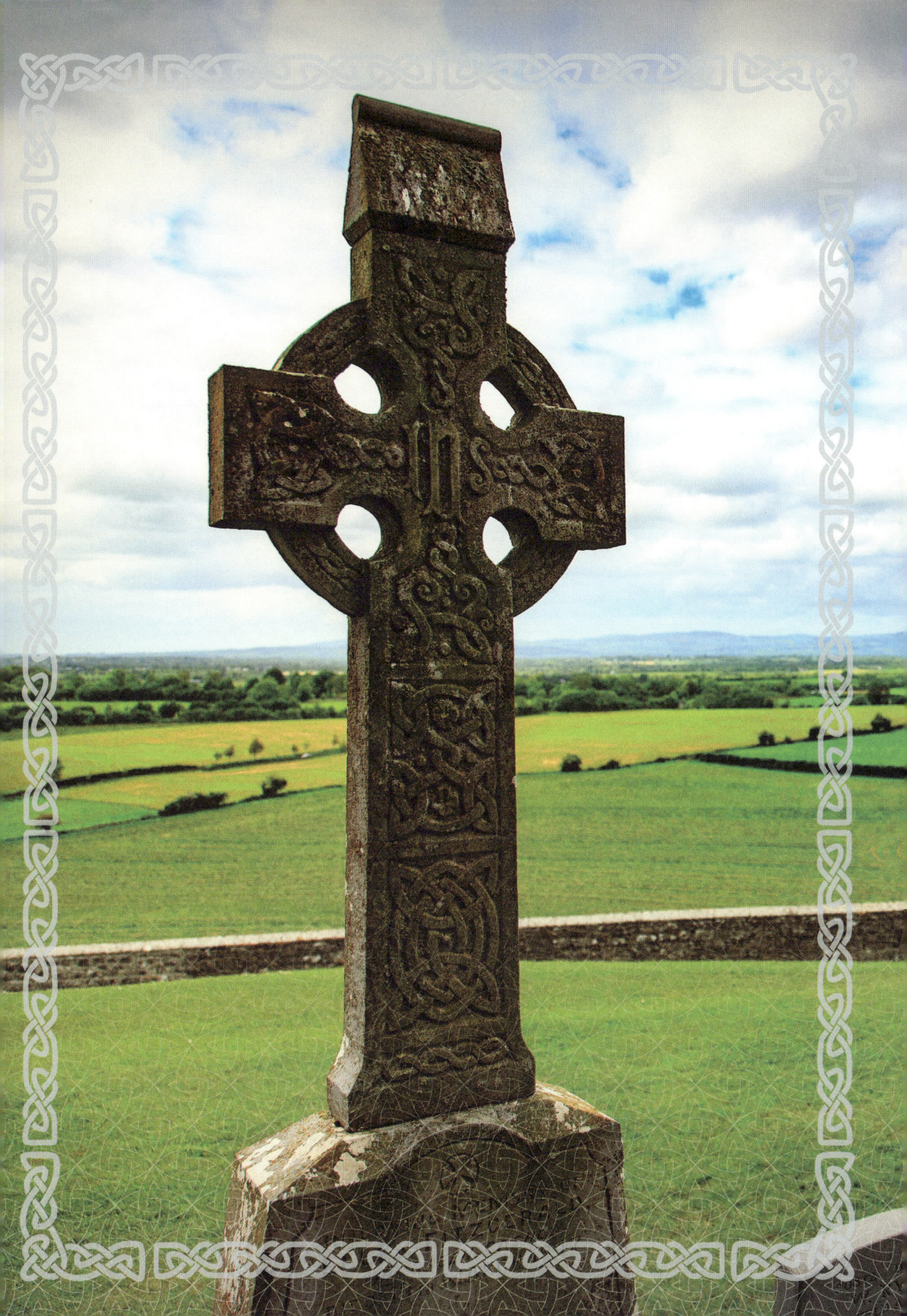

## Celtic Cross Spell to Make a Decision

If you have some kind of dilemma and you are not sure which way to turn, this simple spell can help you to come to a decision. You will need a picture or drawing of a Celtic cross and a small feather. Hold the feather to your heart and say:

⌘

*Pretty plume taking flight*

*Help me make the choice that's right*

Now concentrate on your dilemma and hold the feather over the cross. With your eyes closed, let the feather drop and see where it lands. Whatever part of the cross it lands on should determine your decision:

**Body of Cross** – stay rooted and do nothing for now. All will be revealed in time

**North** – follow your own best interests, be practical and pragmatic

**East** – follow your intellect, think things through carefully, weigh up pros and cons

**South** – follow your heart, do what brings you joy, live passionately

**West** – follow your dreams, go where they take you, trust in your talents

## Meeting of the Ways Spell for Reconciliation

You can also use the symbolism of the Celtic Cross to bring about a reconciliation with someone you've lost touch with. Take an image of the cross and meditate on it for a few minutes—a Celtic Cross necklace would be perfect for this spell. Think of the person you wish to be back in contact with and say the following incantation as you gaze at the cross:

⌘

*I saw you last at the parting of the ways*

*From there you left my side*

*I call you now, to the meeting of the ways*

*In lasting friendship to abide.*

Keep the cross with you and on a daily basis, touch it and say the name of your friend three times.

## In My End is My Beginning

Spirals are a popular Celtic design, because they have neither a defined end or beginning, but can be followed from either the centre or the outer limits and back again, like a labyrinth. Spiral spells are easy to cast and will look pretty on your altar too. All you will need are thirteen stones or pebbles, a slip of paper and a pen. You can use a spiral spell for both manifestation and banishing. Simply write your goal or objective on the piece of paper, fold it in half and place it beneath a stone, saying:

*Such is my intention*. This stone is now your Intention Stone so try to choose one that is easily identifiable from the rest.

To *manifest* your goal, place the rest of the stones in a spiral moving in a clockwise direction, making a clockwise spiral, with your intention stone at the centre. Alternatively, to *banish* something from your life, create a spiral in an anti-clockwise direction, using the intention stone as the final stone at the outer limits of the spiral, thus moving it away from you.

## The Keek Stone

The keek stone is a scrying stone which was traditionally used by Pictish women and Druids as a tool of foresight. It is small and round, with a hole in the middle, hence it is sometimes known as a holey stone. To find a keek stone by the side of a loch is said to be lucky as it will protect the finder from all harm if they carry it with them. Such stones were threaded with string and worn around the neck as talismans.

Women would sit by the side of the loch and look through the hole of the keek stone to scry in the waters beyond. The hole would act as a way to focus attention and filter the images and insights. The Brahan Seer was Scotland's answer to Merlin. He used a keek stone to tell the future, but so scandalous were his predictions that he was taken up on a charge of witchcraft and burned in a barrel at Chanonry Point in Inverness. Today there is a memorial stone there to commemorate him. These days we can use keek stones without fear. They are however, notoriously hard to find, but you can always make your own.

### HOW TO MAKE AND USE A KEEK STONE

To make your own holey stone you will need some modelling clay that fires in a conventional oven, such as Fimo. Choose a colour that appeals to you, or one that looks pebble-like, such as grey or brown. You will also need a piece of string or ribbon, some incense, a rolling pin and a dolly peg. First work the clay in your hands until it is malleable. Next roll it out into a small circle, about the size of a large pebble. Be sure not to roll it too thin – it needs to resemble a pebble. Now using the head of the dolly peg, carefully push a hole through the middle of the clay to create a keek stone. Bake in the oven as directed. Once cooled, thread the keek stone onto the ribbon and pass it through incense smoke to bless it and cleanse it.

To use the stone for scrying, hold a question in your mind then peer through the stone, preferable looking out over water. Alternatively, you can peer through the keek stone into incense smoke. Use your intuition to decipher what images you see in the water or smoke. As with any kind of divination tool, scrying with a keek stone takes practice, so don't be downhearted if you find it difficult at first. Just keep on practicing.

## Blessing of the Four Winds

This simple spell calls on the four winds to bring their blessings into your life. It is best performed out of doors. Light a stick of your favourite incense and face east. Wave the incense and use your hand to pull the smoke towards you as you say:

⌘

***Blessings of East and Air surround me,***

***Powers of communication and creativity all around me***

Face south and repeat the process saying:

⌘

***Blessings of South and Fire surround me***

***Powers of love, passion and adventure all around me***

Face west, pull the incense smoke towards you and say:

⌘

*Blessings of West and Water surround me*

*Powers of intuition and ambition all around me*

Finally, face north, repeat the process and say:

⌘

*Blessings of North and Earth surround me*

*Powers of abundance and growth all around me*

Finish off the spell by dampening the ground with water and staking the incense stick in the earth as you say:

⌘

*As I am blessed by the four winds,*

*So I leave this blessing in return*

*Blessed Be.*

# The Big Grey Man of Ben MacDhui

The mountain of Ben MacDhui in the Cairngorms is said to be home to the Big Grey Man, or *Am Fear Liath Mor*. He is a malevolent creature who dislikes people, and he will do his best to scare them away. Legend states that he prowls the peaks and mountain passes looking for mountaineers and hill walkers so that he can use his presence to intimidate them and make them flee the mountain. Although few have actually seen him, many people have reported feeling a dark threatening presence while in the Cairngorms and on Ben MacDhui in particular. Unlike his mountain cousins in other parts of the world, such as Big Foot and the Yeti, The Big Grey Man isn't covered in fur but is thought to be a very tall and skinny man, so it could be that this legend came about before people understood the phenomenon of the Brocken Spectre. Whatever the truth of it may be, it pays to keep your wits about you when traversing the Highland mountains!

# Conclusion

## Mar sin leibh an-drasta!

***Goodbye for now!***

I hope that you have enjoyed this little book of all things Celtic! In it I have attempted to whet your appetite with history, mythology and magic. Although the Celts originated as a very Euro-centric culture, their influence is now felt globally and many people all over the world have a Celtic heritage and ancestry. This is something that connects us all, for we are all a part of one big Clan – the Clan of the Celts. I trust that you have been inspired to learn more about your own links with the Celts and their influence on your country and culture, wherever you might live.

Remember that the past is always present, and you can tap into the power of Celtic mysticism whenever you want to. Bring the power of the Celts into your daily life by playing bagpipe music, wearing a kilt, observing Burns Night and live your life like a modern Warrior Poet, regardless of gender. Be inspired by your ancestors, knowing that you are the current thread in a much larger tapestry of life. You can never be Clan-less for your ancestors are watching over you. If you are tempted to visit any of the special places I have mentioned in this book, I trust that the magic you find there will stay with you for the rest of your days. May the road always rise to meet you and the path be smoothed before you.

*Mar sin leibh an-drasta* or goodbye for now.

May Celtic blessings rain down upon you, until our next merry meeting!

**Marie Bruce x**

# Further Reading

***Celtic Wisdom*** by Andy Baggot (Piatkus, 1999)

***Scotland: Myths & Legends*** by Beryl Beare (Lomond Books, 1996)

***William Wallace: the man and the myth*** by Chris Brown (The History Press, 2014)

***King and Outlaw: the real Robert the Bruce*** by Chris Brown (The History Press, 2018)

***Scottish Witchcraft*** by Raymond Buckland (Llewellyn, 1991)

***By Oak, Ash and Thorn*** by D J Conway (Llewellyn, 1994)

***Celtic Mythology*** by Arthur Cotterell (Anness, 2000)

***Consider the Lilies*** by Iain Crichton Smith (Orion, 2001)

***The Jacobite Cause*** by Bruce Lenman (Richard Drew Publishing, 1986)

***Scotland: A Concise History*** by Fitzroy Maclean (Thames & Hudson, 2019)

***Encyclopaedia of Celtic Wisdom*** by Caitlin Matthews (Rider, 2001)

***The Quest for the Green Man*** by John Matthews (Octopus, 2004)

***A Gathering: a personal anthology of Scottish poems*** by Alexander Mccall Smith (Birlinn 2018)

***The Silver Bough*** by F. Marian McNeill (William Maclellan, 1968)

***The 21 Lessons of Merlyn*** by Douglas Monroe (Llewellyn, 2002)

***A Year of Scottish Poems*** by Gaby Morgan (Macmillan, 2020)

***A History of Scotland*** by Neil Oliver (Weidenfeld & Nicolson, 2009)

***An Anthology of Scottish Folk Tales*** – various authors (The History Press, 2019)

# Acknowledgments

I am frequently asked where I find my inspiration and I always reply that inspiration is all around us, every day, providing we are actively looking for it! That said, there are several people without whom this book would not have been possible and who I would like to thank. First and foremost, the team at Arcturus, who have given me the opportunity to revisit the topic of Celtic magic and folklore once again, knowing that it is very close to my heart. Also, thanks to my mother, Jacqueline, for her continued love and support and for occasionally being my PA for the day!

Secondly, I must give extra special thanks to my Bannockburn friend, Bob Beverage, for his military knowledge of bagpipes and pipers in history, and for pointing me in the right direction. I first met Bob in 2000 when he was a tour guide in the town of Stirling. He looked magnificent in a traditional tartan, Braveheart style! We have remained friends ever since. He is one of the funniest men I have ever known. Thank you so much for your help with this book Bob.

I would also like to thank my tutors in Advanced Creative Writing and Gothic Literature at The University of Oxford – Louis Greenberg, Octavia Cox and Elizabeth Garner. It has been a great joy to learn from such dedicated professors, who have all helped me to further hone my craft as an author. My time at Oxford will continue to inform all of my writing ventures going forward, as it has done with this book, so thank you for sharing your expertise so generously.

Then there are my boys, Seamus, Hamish, Ally and Davy, who introduced me to the joys of a Highland adventure, which involved climbing a treehouse in the Blackmuir Woods, navigating rope ladders, ropes, planks, a zip-wire and a couple of rambunctious stags! I had the best time in the woods with my boys, playing leapfrog and rounders in the autumn leaves, and I will always be grateful to have met them. I am very proud of the men they have become, each one serving our country in his own way, as soldiers, a teacher and a postman. Our fellowship holds a special place in my heart and always will.

Scotland as always remains the predominant influence in much of my writing and this book is no different. Many of the meditations that appear here are based on my own experiences in the Highlands, including the time in 2019 when I got hopelessly lost on a mountain in Glencoe, during a storm with 80-miles-per-hour winds! Fun. I used this experience as the basis for the meditation, *A Winter Song of Snowflakes*, relocating it to the mountain of Ben Cruachan, which I have also visited, and which is said to be where the Cailleach lives. Loch Ness is also a very special place to me and so I set the *Unburden Your Heart at Urquart* meditation there as it seemed the most fitting place to lay down one's troubles and heartaches. However, Nessie's appearance was a surprise, even to me! Of course, I was always going to include my heroes and heroines, the Good King, Robert the Bruce, William Wallace and Rob Roy, plus strong women of history like Boudicca, Isabella MacDuff and Marjorie Bruce. How could I not? They guide me and inspire me every day.

Not all the inspiration for this book is Scottish and the *Monk's Crossing* meditation was in fact based on a rather spooky experience I had one night, at a place called Stocksbridge Bypass on the A616, where I had to stop the car to allow for dozens of ghostly monks to cross the road in front of me! It was a wonderful, spooky experience and a very ghostly scene which I wanted to include in the book, turning them into Druid monks. The A616 is a notoriously haunted spot, so if you ever go there, expect the unexpected! Love to you all, Marie x

# A Celtic Blessing

*May you always walk in sunshine,*

*May you never want for more,*

*And may angels rest their wings,*

*Right beside your door.*